A Taste of Norway

A Cookbook based on Nature's own Ingredients

Arne Brimi and Bengt Wilson

A Taste of Norway

A Cookbook based on Nature's own Ingredients

Norwegian University Press

All pictures in this book are taken with *Fuji Chrome Professional Film.*
Layout and Cover Design: *Jan Ole Norum*
Cover Photography: *Bengt Wilson*
Food Photography: *Bengt Wilson*
Translation and Adaptarion: *Melody Favish*
Typesettinged and paste-up: *Reclamo Grensen a.s*
Printed in Norway by: *Moestue Bøker A.s, Oslo, 1990*

Contents

Introduction

The food I make has its roots in the traditions of my home district, the Otta valley of central Norway. I believe it is important to make use of both local traditions and local products and to use those as departure points for developing new dishes.

Nature's kitchen preserves the fresh flavors of the raw materials. These flavors are enhanced by the use of other gifts of nature, herbs and spices.

As a cook, I have had two important sources of inspiration. The first is the landscape surrounding my home area. I love being outdoors, and I feel very much at home in the mountains, which have an appeal that is hard to explain. I enjoy both hunting and fishing. These activities give me both strength and inspiration. I have even learned to recognize wild plants that I can use in my kitchen. By learning more about nature, I have come to respect it and to feel responsible for preserving it.

My second source of inspiration taught me to appreciate the first in a new way. In France, every region has its own food traditions. While working there, I learned to appreciate the special products of every district, including my own, and to use them with pride.

Just as the French both preserve their old traditions and develop new ones for the modern kitchen, I propose to do the same for Norwegian food. There is no need to copy the French or anyone else. Our food must be developed on our own terms and in our own kitchens. Norwegian food can stand on its own.

Here in Norway, we have access to many kinds of top-quality products. Working in French kitchens has taught me to use them wisely and has given me the self-confidence to try unconventional methods of preparation.

Many of the recipes in this book can be used with a variety of raw materials. I think it can serve both as a cookbook and as a source of inspiration in both large and small kitchens.

The World Championship for Chefs in Lyons in 1987 was both a high point and a challenge. Next in line is the Culinary Olympics in Frankfurt in late 1988. I would not have been able to participate at either of these without the inspiration and support of many people around me.

Fossheim Turisthotell has given me free hands all the time I have been there. Few places would give a young chef such an opportunity, and I am very grateful for the help and support of all my co-workers. With their help, I have developed my own style of cooking, which I call "Nature's Kitchen." All the pictures in this book were taken at Fossheim.

Throughout my life, Grete Sjurgard has been very special to me. She helped me to develop as a person, and she encouraged me in my work with her enthusiasm and her constructive criticism. I learned from her that the simplest way is often the best, and thanks to her, I have found the means to express myself.

In writing this book, Aase Strømstad solved many problems with the recipes. Her experience and knowledge have been of great help.

In addition, my collaboration with Bengt Wilson has been essential for the making of this book.

Lom, Norway
Arne Brimi
June, 1988

P.S. When using the recipes in this book, follow either the cup version or the metric one. Do not try to mix the two.

Fish

Fishing is my kind of recreation. Whether by the side of a lake or a river, I enjoy it fully, preferably with a pole and line. And fish always tastes better when it is cooked outdoors.

9

The most important fish in my district in inland Norway is trout. There are other kinds of fish, but the trout in the mountain lakes have always been considered the best.

I usually get fish from Tesse, the largest lake in Lom. There are more than 20 stone age settlements around Tesse. The oldest is thought to be about 5000–6000 years old, while most range from 2000–4000 years old.

These settlements indicate that Tesse has been an important source of fish for thousands of years. We know that King Olaf the Holy gave Tesse to Torgeir the Elder at Garmo, as compensation for allowing himself to be christened, and for promising to build a church on his farm. This is mentioned in Snorre's sagas of the Norwegian kings and dates from 1021, when King Olaf, known also as St. Olaf, travelled through the valley in his efforts to spread Christianity throughout Norway.

Torgeir the Elder kept his word. The people of Garmo still have the fishing rights for Tesse. The church that he built now stands at the open-air museum at Maihaugen, near Lillehammer.

The catch varies from year to year, but 8–10 tons was normal until recently. Regulation has reduced the water a bit. Fishing is permitted all summer until spawning time, and then there are 10 days of fishing at the end of October. The last fish of the season are often made into *rakefisk*, which are then ready just in time for Christmas.

Tesse fish are especially good, just right for *rakefisk*. Good *rakefisk* should preserve the natural flavor of the trout and not be too salty. The flesh should be smooth enough to be spread with a knife, and the fish itself should be odorless.

There are many opinions as to how *rakefisk* should be made. It is a dish that takes time and practice to get just right. I learned to make it from Eli Brimi, the hostess at Brimi Mountain Lodge at Tesse.

Salmon and sea trout

Salmon is the aristocrat of Norwegian rivers. Who hasn't been fascinated by salmon fishing or by the great journeys salmon make from sea to river to spawn?

Salmon is one of the major culinary highpoints we can offer, and it is one of the best fish there is. *Gravlaks*, marinated salmon, is considered on par with goose liver and Russian caviar, while Ocean trout is a close second. Both salmon and trout can be prepared in much the same manner.

Poached Salmon or Trout

Whether you plan to serve poached fish for dinner or you prefer to serve it cold, you need a good bouillon as a basis. Cooks usually call this liquid a court bouillon, which means seasoned water for cooking fish. Fish should simmer, never boil.

The most commonly used liquid for poaching fish is just water and salt. Some use lemon as well, but the fish will taste even better with a few additional ingredients, such as wine, vegetables and herbs.

BOUILLON FOR SALMON OR TROUT

3 quarts (liters) water
1 ½ tbsp salt
1 lemon, peeled and pitted
6–8 whole white peppercorns
1 bay leaf stalks from one bunch parsley

1 small leek (see Appendix)
¾ cup (200 ml) white wine

Bring to a boil and let simmer 15–20 minutes before adding fish.

Salmon Soup

3 cups (800 ml) salmon broth (cook salmon
　　head, bones and trimmings in court
　　bouillon, then strain)
$^1\!/_2$ cup (100 ml) white wine
$^1\!/_2$ cup (100 ml) crème fraîche (see Appendix)
salt
2 small carrots, in matchstick pieces
$^2\!/_3$ cup (100 g) small broccoli florets
$^2\!/_3$ cucumber, in matchstick pieces
8–10 ounces (200–300 g) skinless and
　　boneless salmon
dill

Bring salmon broth and wine to a boil. Beat in
crème fraîche. Salt to taste. Blanch vegetables
separately in a small amount of water. Cut salmon
into cubes and divide among four warm soup
bowls. Pour hot soup over the fish, so that it will
be cooked by it. Place some of the vegetables in
each bowl. Garnish with dill. Serves 4.

Salmon Soup with Chives

8 thin slices of salmon fillet, about 2 ounces
　　(60–70 g) each
3 cups (800 ml) fish broth
juice of $^1\!/_2$ lemon
$^1\!/_2$ cup (100 ml) white wine
1 tbsp unsalted butter
$^1\!/_2$ tsp cornstarch
2 tsp salt
6 tbsp chives

Remove any skin and bones from salmon. Trim
so that all slices are about the same size. Steam
until just done, 1–2 minutes depending upon
thickness.

　　Season fish broth with lemon juice and white
wine. Beat in butter. Stir cornstarch into 2 teaspoons water and add to soup. This prevents the
butter from separating from the broth. Salt to
taste. Pour soup into warm bowls. Add chives and
salmon. Serves 4.

Lyons Salmon

This is a difficult and time-consuming dish to prepare. The philosophy behind it is the same as with everything I make, that the natural flavor of the main ingredient must be dominant, and that everything served with it should enhance the main ingredient. Note that there is almost no salt in this dish. It is a greater challenge to create flavors without salt. In this case, the sorrel, lemon and white wine replace the salt, while the mint tempers the acidity of the sorrel.

If you have the time and energy to try this dish, I can only say that you will enjoy it.

1 salmon, 6–7 lbs (3 kg)

CRAYFISH:
24 crayfish or large shrimp
2 quarts (liters) water
1 ¼ cups (300 ml) Sancerre or other white wine
2 tbs salt
1 bunch dill

Start with the crayfish: Bring the water to a boil, and add white wine, salt and dill. Add crayfish and simmer 8 minutes.

Remove crayfish and cool. Save cooking water for soup.

Shell crayfish, taking care to discard the black vein in the tail. Reserve tails for garnish. Save all edible bits from inside the shell and claws for the mousse. Save front part of shells to hold mousse, and save remaining shells for the stock.

Clean, wash and fillet the salmon. Remove all bones, using tweezers for those along the central ridge of the fillets.

To remove skin, place fillet, skin side down, on a cutting board. Make a small cut at the tail end, just large enough to slide in a knife. Hold the skin with the fingertips and thumb of one hand, then press the knife diagonally against the skin and peel it off with one movement. Trim the fillet of any small bits of skin, and remove any fat, which is a darker color than the rest of the fish, from the skin side.

Cut four pieces of equal size from the center portion of each fillet. Use remaining fish for the mousse.

FISH STOCK:
crayfish shells
fish bones
salmon head without gills
1 quart (liter) cooking liquid from crayfish
1 ⅓ cups (400 ml) Sancerre or other white wine
2 cups (500 ml) water
2 lemons, peeled and pitted
1 bunch sorrel (remove a few leaves for garnish)
1 bunch mint (remove a few leaves for garnish)
10 shallots
1 large leek (see Appendix)
whole white pepper

Place crayfish shells, thoroughly cleaned and rinsed fish bones and head in a pot. Add crayfish liquid, wine and water. Bring to a boil and skim well. Add remaining ingredients and simmer, over low heat, about 50 minutes. Strain.

The stock should be completely clear and without fat globules. There should be no need for more seasoning.

SALMON MOUSSE:
4 ounces (100 g) boneless salmon
crayfish meat from claws and front shell
3 tbsp whipping cream
scant ½ cup (100 ml) white wine
4 egg whites
1 tsp salt

Purée in a food processor or blender. Press through a sieve and spoon into crayfish shells.

Steam fish slices and stuffed shells, covered, on a rack over boiling water. The salmon fillets need 4 minutes to cook to "medium," while the crayfish need 1 more minute. The mousse should puff like a soufflé.

TO SERVE:
1 lb (500 g) carrots, cut into balls
8 scallions
8 ounces (250 g) mushrooms
2–4 truffles (optional)

Cook carrots until crisp. Dip the scallions in boiling water for a few seconds. Place 1 piece of fish and 2 crayfish shells filled with salmon mousse in each deep plate. Pour over hot bouillon and garnish each with 2 crayfish tails, several mushroom slics, carrot balls, a scallion and strips of truffle. Sprinkle with chopped sorrell and a few mint leaves. Serves 8.

Poaching of Fish to Serve Cold

Make a court bouillon (see Page 10) and cool completely. Clean fish and place in the bouillon. Bring to a boil. Reduce heat and simmer until fish is almost done. Remove from heat and cool in cooking liquid. Small fish weighing 8–10 ounces (200–300 g) need no more time than it takes for the liquid to reach a boil. Larger fish, such as a salmon or sea trout, weighing about 4 lbs (2 kg), need to simmer about 15–20 minutes.

Salmon Pockets Stuffed with Shrimp

This delicious dish is best served directly on the plate.

> 1 ⅓ lb (600 g) salmon fillet
> 4 tbsp chopped cooked shrimp
> 2–3 tbsp crème fraîche (see Appendix)
> 2–3 tbsp white wine
> 1 tbsp chopped dill
> salt
> 1 egg white
> 2 tbsp clarified butter (the clear top layer of
>   melted butter)

Preheat oven to 450°F (225°C).

Clean and trim salmon. Remove all bones and skin as described in the previous recipe. Cut 8 thin slices of equal size from the fillet. Place half on a greased baking sheet.

Cook shrimp with crème fraîche and white wine about a minute, to make a smooth mixture. Add dill and salt to taste. Place a spoonful of shrimp mixture on each salmon fillet. Brush edges with egg white and place another piece of salmon on top. Press edges to seal. Brush with clarified butter and bake 3–4 minutes.

Serve immediately with fresh vegetables and a sauce made with stock cooked from shrimp shells and flavored with chopped dill, or with Sandefjord butter. Serves 4.

SANDEFJORD BUTTER

Named after the coastal fishing town of Sandefjord, this is Norway's classic fish sauce. It suits all types of poached or baked fish.

> ⅓ cup (100 ml) whipping cream
> 1 cup (250 g) unsalted butter
> 2–3 tbsp chopped parsley or chives
> salt

Bring cream to a boil. Beat in pats of butter. Whisk vigorously, until sauce is light and smooth. Do not boil.

Just before serving, add parsley or chives. Salt to taste.

Steamed Mountain Trout with Mint Sauce

2 trout, about 8 ounces (250 g) each

FISH STOCK:
skin, head without gills, bones
about 2 cups (500 ml) water
2 bay leaves, 1 carrot
¹/₂ leek (see Appendix)
³/₄ cup (200 ml) white wine
juice of ¹/₂ lemon

SAUCE:
1 ¹/₄ cups (300 ml) fish stock
³/₄ cup (200 ml) whipping cream
¹/₂ cup (100 ml) fresh mint leaves
2 tsp arrowroot or cornstarch mixed with
    1 tbsp cold water
up to 4 tbsp white wine

FOR COOKING THE FISH:
1 quart (liter) water, 1 tbsp salt
¹/₂ cup (100 ml) white wine
juice of ¹/₂ lemon

Clean and fillet the trout. Remove as many small bones as possible and peel off the skin.

Rinse the heads, skin and bones well, and place in a pot with water to cover.

Bring to a boil and skim. Add bay leaves, leek, carrot, wine and lemon juice. Simmer, uncovered, 45–60 minutes, skimming as necessary. Strain stock and reduce to about ¹/₄ – 1 cup (3 dl). Add cream and cook, uncovered, several minutes. Chop mint finely and add. Thicken sauce with arrowroot and add white wine and salt to taste. Keep warm.

Bring water, salt, white wine and lemon juice to a boil. Steam fish on a rack over mixture for 5–6 minutes.

Divide the sauce among four heated plates and place a fillet on each. Garnish with cucumber tournettes, which have been blanched for a few seconds before serving.

Serve with bread. Serves 4 as a first course.

As a main dish, allow two fillets per person. Served with potatoes and cooked vegetables.

Trout with Red Currants

4 pieces of center-cut trout fillet, about 5
    ounces (150 g) each
1 leek (see Appendix)
$\frac{1}{2}$ cucumber
1 bunch parsley
2 carrots, shredded
salt
fresh mint
$\frac{2}{3}$ cup (150 ml) red currants
white wine
2 tbsp unsalted butter

Remove any bones and skin from the fish. Preheat oven to 450°F (225°C).

Finely chop leek, cucumber and parsley and
mix with carrot. Place vegetables in a baking dish
and sprinkle with salt, chopped mint and red currants. Add white wine, until it covers about $\frac{3}{4}$
of the vegetables. Dot with butter and place fish
on top. Cover with foil and bake about 35 minutes. Serve immediately with fresh rolls. Serves 4.

Or you can do this: On the day before serving,
place fish in a marinade of white wine with some
shredded carrot, leek and mint and refrigerate at
least 12 hours. Wrap fillets, along with vegetables
and a pat of butter in individual parchment paper
packets and bake at 400°F (200°C) for 15 minutes.

Warm-Smoked Trout

1 trout, about 3 lbs ($\frac{1}{2}$ – 1 kg)
coarse salt

Clean and rinse trout well. Sprinkle cavity with salt. Place on a tray with some salt underneath and sprinkle top of fish with more salt. Refrigerate 24 hours. Wipe off salt. Smoke at 275–350°F (140–180°C) for 1 hour.

Serve with sour cream, scrambled eggs and flatbread.

Fermented Fish

Rakefisk (fermented fish) is a Norwegian delicacy, but for some, it is an acquired taste.

Use very fresh fish. Wash well and rinse in several changes of water. Dry with paper towels. The fish must be completely free of blood.

Layer fish in a small wooden barrel with the cavities diagonally upward. Sprinkle a tablespoon of salt and a teaspoon of sugar on each layer. Place a weight on top and let stand 2–3 days, the first day at room temperature, to start the fermentation process. Refrigerate. Keep the lid tightly fastened.

A brine will form after 2–3 days. If it does not cover the fish completely, make additional brine: 3 quarts (liters) water, $\frac{1}{2}$ cup (100 ml) salt and 2 teaspoons sugar. The fish is ready after 5–6 weeks. It is important to change the brine if it becomes cloudy. Use the above recipe. *Rakefisk* is served with *lefse* (potato pancake) or flatbread and butter. Beer is a must, and some enjoy a chaser of aquavit with it, as well.

Fresh Fish Prepared Outdoors

Fishing can be a passion for some, for others it is a means of relaxation. I can think of no better way to alleviate stress than to enjoy a fish dinner outdoors on a warm summer evening. Whether you have only a few fish, or you have caught many, you can have a wonderful meal.

There is always something special about enjoying the fruits of one's labors, and no fish tastes better than the one you caught yourself and prepared outdoors, just off the hook. With a little imagination, it is possible to prepare fish in a number of ways, even without a kitchen.

The most popular way to prepare fish outdoors is to cook it over an open fire. Remember to bring aluminum foil, butter and salt.

When the coals are glowing, place some salt, butter and green herbs, such as sorrel, parsley and chives, in the cavity of the fish and wrap well in foil. Place in the coals and cook 10–12 minutes, according to size. It tastes great straight from the fire, but with a little sour cream and bread, you have a memorable meal.

Another idea is to smoke the fish over the coals. Then it is wise to salt the fish a little in advance. Place a twig or two crosswise in the cavity to hold it open and hang about 12 inches (30 cm) over the coals. Place fresh juniper branches on the fire, not too much at once but enough to produce a steady amount of smoke all the time. Let the fish hang 20–30 minutes. Then it cooks as it is being smoked. The juniper gives the fish a piquant flavor. Serve with sour cream and bread.

If you have a cabin with a fireplace, you can use the chimney for smoking. The procedure is basically the same. Make sure you have a good pile of glowing coals and hang the fish at the top of the chimney. Use juniper if you can. How long the fish has to hang varies with size of the fish, the length of the chimney, and so forth, but it is easy to check the fish while it is being smoked.

If you are at a cabin, you usually can find a little flatbread and something cold to drink to go with the fish.

Baked Cold-Smoked Fish

Proceed as for smoked fish (see Page 18), but smoke it in a regular cold-smoking oven at 90°F (30°C). Wrap fish in aluminum foil and bake in a 300°F (150°C) oven for 1¼ hours. Cool in foil.

Serve in same manner as warm-smoked fish.

The fish should be easy to cut with a spoon and fork, not too salty, and with a slightly smoky taste.

Cold-Smoked Trout

For a fish weighing about ½ lb (250 g):

Sprinkle the fish with salt, both inside the cavity and outside. Refrigerate two days before smoking in a regular cold-smoking oven. Ask your butcher to smoke the fish for you. To give a precise amount of salt is difficult, but it is better with too little than too much. After two days of salting, the fish has a mildly salty flavor, even with only a little salt.

Traditional accompaniments for smoked trout are scrambled eggs, sour cream and flatbread or regular bread.

Marinated Trout or Salmon

There are as many ways to marinate fish as there are cooks. Most like to keep their own special touches a secret.

Even though marinated fish is served year round, it tastes best in the summer. Then we can get both fresh fish and fresh dill.

Salmon and trout are not the only fish that can be marinated. Mackerel and herring are just as good, and the method is the same. In other districts freshwater fish, such as whitefish and char, are used.

Marinated salmon, *gravlaks*, came to us from Sweden, where it is considered a delicacy on line with Russian caviar and goose liver. That sounds strange to us, since salmon is so easy to get in Norway.

Do not wash fish that is going to be marinated. Just dry it well with paper towels. It is a good idea to freeze the fish for 24 hours before preparation, just in case it has any small parasites lurking about. You also can freeze the fish after it has been marinated. It is a good idea to freeze the fish when it has been marinated just right, to stop the process.

Don't try to marinate fish that are too small. You need relatively large fillets for the best results.

For each lb (500 g) fish you will need:
⅓ cup (75 ml) salt
⅓ cup (75 ml) sugar
about 20 white peppercorns, crushed
dill

Fillet and bone the fish. Dry the fillets well.

Mix salt, sugar and pepper and rub into both sides of fillets. Place several fronds of dill in the bottom of a dish large enough to hold an entire fillet. Place one fillet on dill, skin side down. Sprinkle generously with chopped dill. Place second fillet on top, skin side up. Refrigerate for 2 days, turning several times during the marinating process. Serve marinated fish with coarse bread and mustard sauce.

MUSTARD SAUCE
*3 tbsp Dijon-style mustard (do not use "hot
    dog" mustard)*
1 tbsp sugar
½ tbsp vinegar
salt and finely crushed white peppercorns
3 tbsp oil
finely chopped dill
Beat together until emulsified.
You can make a lighter sauce with the following:
mayonnaise
mustard
buttermilk
finely chopped dill
sherry

Meat

Norwegian lamb spend the summer and early fall eating salty mountain grasses. No wonder the meat is so good.

23

Stock

Good stock or broth is basic to the classic kitchen. It is impossible to make good sauces or soups without it. Many people think it is time-consuming to make stock, while others think it is complicated. Of course it takes time, but time and love are very important ingredients in cooking!

There's no doubt that the result produced with a good stock is completely different from that with bouillon cubes. Too many cooks, both at home and in restaurants, rely on them. It's true that making stock is more work than art, but anyone who enjoys making good food ought to take the trouble to make stock.

Stock freezes well, so it's a good idea to make a big pot.

My brown stock recipe uses veal, beef, moose or reindeer bones. Veal and reindeer are best. Classic recipes use veal.

This is a general recipe for stock, meant as a guideline. You can vary herbs to suit your own taste.

It is only natural for me to use juniper in stock made from reindeer. For other kinds, I use other seasonings. The amount of vegetables used can vary.

I usually cook stock 4–5 hours. That's a bit on the long side. 2–3 hours of cooking produce a mild, tasty stock, which can be used in soups and mild sauces.

Additional simmering time concentrates the stock. Then the bones ought to be removed. The longer the stock cooks, the more intense the flavor becomes.

I also make stock from poultry and fish. For a light stock, do not brown the bones.

Brown Stock

9 lbs (4 kg) bones

2 onions
1 leek (see Appendix)
3 carrots
¼ celeriac or 3 stalks celery
6–7 bay leaves
½ tbsp whole white peppercorns
1 tsp thyme
salt
2 tbsp tomato paste, optional
1 bottle red wine, optional

Preheat oven to 450°F (225°C). Chop or saw the bones into 2 inches (5 cm) pieces. Dice vegetables. Place bones and vegetables in a roasting pan with a small amount of water. Roast one hour, or until the bones are nicely browned, adding additional water if necessary.

Transfer bones and vegetables to a pot. Add water to cover. Bring slowly to a boil, skim well and add remaining ingredients, including tomato paste and red wine, if desired. Simmer, uncovered, 4–5 hours. Skim several times.

Strain stock and cool. When the stock is completely cold, it is easy to remove the fat which forms on top.

Freeze any stock that will not be used right away.

SEASONING VARIATIONS
Reindeer
15 juniper berries or ¾ cup (200 ml)
wild raspberries
Moose
juniper berries, young juniper shoots, lingonberries
Deer
same as for moose
Lamb
basil or rosemary

Stock from game birds

I make stock from the bones and giblets of these birds. I season it with crowberries, blueberries or lingonberries.

These birds have a wonderful, natural flavor.

Boiled Meat and Soup

Boiled meat and soup is a traditional dish throughout Norway. Before refrigeration, it was usual to preserve meat by salting. Normal preparation then involved soaking and boiling. That resulted in both a main dish and soup. Soup, or "spoon food", was a very important part of the diet. Food had to be nourishing, especially for that large segment of the population that did hard physical labor. These soups were often made with barley or dried peas. Both have to soak overnight before cooking. The soaking water from peas must be discarded, but the barley water can be used in the soup.

This dish can be varied almost endlessly, with regard to both meat and vegetables. Several kinds of meat can be cooked together, and it tastes especially good when a hambone is added.

Since the meat will be cooked slowly in liquid, it is practical to use tougher cuts, such as arm, chuck or short ribs. Bones just add to the flavor.

All kinds of meat will do, but pork should be salted beforehand. Other kinds of meat should be used fresh. Years ago, people used whatever they had, and that could be anything from small birds to rabbits. Game adds a delicious flavor to the soup.

This recipe is based on fresh meat, and for that reason, fresh vegetables are used, instead of dried peas or barley.

Place meat and bones in a large pot and fill with water to cover. Salt and bring slowly to a boil. Skim well. Add remaining ingredients and simmer $1\frac{1}{2}$ hours.

Slice meat and serve with vegetables on the side. Strain the soup and serve. Spoon off fat, if necessary.

Serve the soup clear or with vegetables such as cabbage and carrots. Serves 4.

Many are probably familiar with these small dumplings, called *krummer*. They were used a lot in soups years ago.

DUMPLINGS
1 tbsp flour
small amount of milk
1 egg
salt

Stir flour into milk and add egg. For especially fine dumplings, use two eggs. Place them directly in the soup with a tablespoon. Do not allow the soup to boil or they will disintegrate. Simmer for a few minutes until done.

If marrow bones are cooked with the soup, they also should be served. You might want to wrap them in cheesecloth during cooking, to prevent the marrow from seeping out.

$2\frac{1}{2}$ lbs ($1\frac{1}{4}$ kg) meat
marrow bones (if meat is boneless)
water to cover
4 tsp salt
4 carrots
1 leek (see Appendix)
8–10 whole white peppercorns
1 bay leaf
2 tsp thyme
$\frac{1}{4}$ head cabbage
$\frac{1}{2}$ small rutabaga
parsley

Lamb

"Norwegian lamb, world-class meat" is the slogan of the Norwegian Meat Information Board, and we have to agree with that. Considering that the animals have eaten the best of wild grasses during the summer, the meat has to be succulent and of top quality.

Stuffed Leg of Lamb with Sherry Sauce

1 leg of lamb, 4 to 4½ lbs (2 kg)

SAUCE:
3⅓ cups (800 ml) lamb stock
cornstarch or arrowroot
¾ cup (200 ml) whipping cream
salt
pepper
½ cup (100 ml) sherry

STUFFING:
½ onion
½ leek (see Appendix)
1 small bunch parsley
4–5 stalks celery
½ green or red pepper
oil
2 tsp salt
1 tsp pepper

Ask your butcher to bone the lamb, or do it yourself, cutting as close to the bones as possible.

Make stock from the bones (Page 24). Thicken slightly with cornstarch or arrowroot. Add cream and season with salt and pepper to taste. Just before serving, add sherry for a smooth, balanced flavor.

Preheat oven to 425°F (225°C). Finely chop vegetables and brown in oil. Season stuffing to taste and spread over lamb. Roll, and tie at equal intervals with cotton string. Brown leg of lamb in a large pan. Insert a meat thermometer and roast about 45 minutes, until internal temperature registers 130–140°F (55–60°C). Remove from oven and let rest 10 minutes. Slice thinly and serve.

Serve with cauliflower, Brussels sprouts, broccoli or carrots and duchesse potatoes (Page 82). Serves 6–8.

Buttermilk-Marinated Lamb

This is an example of both tradition and modern thinking. It's a simple recipe with a good result.

1 leg of lamb, 4 to 4½ lbs (2 kg)

MARINADE:
1 quart (liter) buttermilk
1 tbsp sugar
1 tbsp salt
1 tbsp thyme
¾ cup (200 ml) red clover heads (see Page 114).

Place leg of lamb in a plastic bag or a tightly fitting container. Mix marinade, pour over lamb and marinate 4 days. If the entire leg is not covered, turn it several times while marinating.

Preheat oven to 400°F (200°C). Wrap leg of lamb in aluminum foil and insert a meat thermometer. Roast until the internal temperature registers 130–140°F (55–60°C), about 60–70 minutes. Remove from oven and let rest 10 minutes.

Slice and serve with the natural juices of the lamb, fresh vegetables and boiled potatoes. This dish can be served cold, with aspic and lingonberries. Serves 6–8.

Boned Saddle of Lamb

*1 saddle of lamb, preferably from
    the autumn, as it is larger
clarified butter or oil*

SAUCE:
*2 cups (500 ml) lamb stock
6 tbsp butter
2–3 tbsp sherry vinegar
2 tsp cornstarch or arrowroot mixed with 1
    tbsp cold water
5–6 tbsp rosé wine*

The saddle yields both the loin strip and the fillet. Bone the saddle and trim meat of all fat, gristle and membrane. Make stock from the bones (see Page 24).

COOKING THE MEAT
Preheat oven to 425°F (225°C). Brown the whole strips of meat and season with salt and pepper. Roast in oven for 5–6 minutes. Allow meat to rest a few minutes before slicing. It is supposed to be pink inside.

Bring the stock to a boil. Beat in butter and season to taste with sherry vinegar and salt. Thicken with cornstarch. Just before serving, add wine for a fresh taste which heightens the flavor of the lamb.

Serve with fresh vegetables, such as snow peas and baby carrots. Buttered tiny new potatoes as well as duchesse potatoes (see Page 82) are good with this dish. Serves 4.

Stuffed Shoulder of Lamb

This dish can be served hot or cold, as a main
dish or as part of a buffet table.

1 small shoulder of lamb
clarified butter or oil

STUFFING:
4 slices day-old white bread, crustless
about $^1/_2$ cup (100 ml) whipping cream
2–3 tbsp finely-chopped green or red pepper
2–3 tbsp finely-chopped leek
2 tbsp finely-chopped celery
rosemary
basil
salt

Ask your butcher to bone the shoulder, or do it
yourself, cutting against the bones. Preheat
oven to 425°F (225°C). Cube bread and mash
with cream. Add remaining ingredients and
mix.

Spread stuffing over meat, roll and tie at even
intervals with cotton string. Brown, then transfer to a rack over a roasting pan. Roast 25–30
minutes. Cool. Serves 4.

To serve hot:
Allow the meat to rest 10 minutes before slicing.
The bones should be saved to make the stock.
Make a sauce seasoned with rosemary and basil.
Serve with potatoes and vegetables.

To serve cold:
Place the sliced roast in an aspic made from 2
parts red currant or other berry wine, 1 part red
wine and gelatine. 2 tbsp powdered gelatine
will stiffen 1 quart (liter) liquid.

28

Marinated Smoked Lamb

1 leg of lamb
2 tbsp salt
1 bottle red wine

Rub lamb with salt and refrigerate 24 hours. Place in a plastic bag with the wine. Tie the bag well and marinate 4–5 days. Have your butcher cold-smoke the lamb.

ROASTING AND SERVING
Preheat oven to 240°F (120°C). Insert a meat thermometer into the thickest part, but not against bone. Roast until internal temperature reaches 130–140°F (55–60°C).

Cool completely and serve with bread and butter and a salad seasoned with thyme and chives. Serves 5–6.

Cold Marinated Lamb

⅔ cup (150 ml) sugar
⅔ cup (150 ml) salt
3 tbsp coarsely ground white pepper
1 large bunch fresh thyme, chopped
1 bunch dill
2 carrots, finely chopped
1 leek, finely chopped
½ celeriac, finely chopped
1 leg of lamb, about 4½ lbs (2 kg), boned
½ bottle red wine
3 tbsp sherry vinegar

Place half the sugar, salt, herbs and vegetables in the bottom of a deep dish. Place the lamb on the mixture and spread the rest of the sugar, etc. over it. Pour over wine and vinegar. Place a 3–lb (1½ kg) weight on the meat and refrigerate. Turn meat over once a day and marinate for 5 days.

Slice very thinly and serve cold with mustard sauce or sour cream seasoned with chopped herbs, and with bread and butter. Serves 8–10 as a first course.

Herb-Stuffed Lamb Roll

Lamb roll can be much more than just a Christmas treat. This roll is especially good in the autumn.

1 lamb flank with ribs
2 tbsp chopped parsley
1 tbsp chopped fresh or ½ tsp dried mint
1 tbsp fresh or ½ tsp dried thyme
sliced mushrooms
salt and pepper
clarified butter or oil

Bone and trim flank to a rectangular shape. Save bones for stock. Trimmings can be used in the stuffing.

Preheat oven to 425°F (225°C). Lay the flank, meaty side up, and distribute stuffing over the meat. Roll up tightly and tie at even intervals with cotton string. Brown, then transfer to a roasting pan. Deglaze pan with water and pour over meat. Roast about 25 minutes, basting often.

Serve with several kinds of fresh vegetables and potatoes. Cook the vegetables in lightly salted water with a pat of butter until crisply tender. Baked creamed potatoes suit this dish well. Serves 4.

Game

Smådalen valley was once the calving place for much of the wild reindeer in southern Norway. There are remains from former hunts all over the area. Whenever I wander through the magnificent landscape, I always feel a great respect for nature, and I get new inspiration for the next time I am in the kitchen.

Hunting

Hunting means a lot to many Norwegians. A week of hunting will often cost more than a trip abroad, but many a hunter feels it's worth the price to enjoy some autumn days with a rifle on his shoulder. Hunting means different things to different people. In number of animals, moose hunting is the most important, while as recreation, all types have the same value.

In Norway, reindeer, moose and deer can be hunted only for a few weeks, so activity is intense while it lasts. Hare and ptarmigan can be hunted for a longer period of time. For those of us who live nearby, that means many fall and winter weekends are devoted to the sport.

As a cook, it is my goal to unite the exclusive products of the forest and mountains with small works of art, both for the eye and the palate. My interest in hunting makes me feel close to nature, and I try to use what nature has taught me in new approaches to the food I make.

Moose

Even though the moose-hunting season is short, not a few tons of moose meat end up in Norwegian freezers. In the past few years, moose have spread out, so they can be hunted just about everywhere in Norway.

In my home area there has also been an increase in the number of moose, so that it is now easier to obtain moose meat. I like to be right out there in the woods with the hunters, to help with the butchering. That way, I get the cuts I like.

Size and age, along with general physical condition, have a lot to say with regard to the quality of the meat. Large animals often have rather coarse meat, and that has to be taken into consideration during preparation. But in the last few years, the average weight per animal has fallen. The best weigh about 350–375 lbs (160–180 kg), but, as mentioned earlier, it still depends upon age and condition. Some years ago, I got an animal weighing over 730 lbs (333 kg). It was at the pinnacle of its career.

Moose has a less characteristic taste than other game. It tastes a lot like beef. I think it is important to consider the special qualities of the raw materials and to use them accordingly. A top round cut is different from an eye of round, for instance, even though both are part of the leg.

It is also important with large animals to divide them logically and naturally. For small varieties of deer, the leg should preferably not be partitioned. With larger animals such as moose, the leg must be partitioned according to the different muscles, so that top round, bottom round, eye of round and sirloin are separated.

TOP ROUND
is the best part of the leg and should be roasted, but it also can also be cut into steaks.

BOTTOM ROUND
also can be roasted, but care must be taken to remove any gristle and membrane. The smaller part of this cut is tougher than the larger and benefits from slow roasting at 250°F (125°C).

SIRLOIN
sits on top of the leg and is probably the tastiest cut. It makes an excellent roast.

EYE OF ROUND
is the toughest part of the leg, even though it looks like a beautiful filet. It can be simmered or salted and made into corned beef.

Moose Steak with Onions and Herb Butter

The strip loin, on the outer part of the saddle, has more taste than the fillet, but it's not quite so tender.

Strip steaks should be thick, juicy and tender. The size may vary, but I think about 6 ounces (180 g) is just right.

How it should be cooked is a matter of taste, but I think most people enjoy their meat cooked to "medium," with a pink center.

> 2–3 large onions
> unsalted butter
> 4 strip steaks, 6 ounces (180 g) each, about
>   1 1/4 inches (3 cm) thick
> clarified butter or oil, salt and pepper

Slice onion and fry in butter until golden, shiny and soft. Set aside while cooking meat.

Heat clarified butter or oil until almost smoking. Place steaks in the pan. Turn after 1 minute and season the cooked side with salt and pepper. Turn steaks again after one more minute and sea-

son the other side. Continue cooking, turning several times, so that the meat does not burn. The steaks are "medium" when pearls of meat juices form on the surfaces, about 3–4 minutes per side. For well done meat, cook 5 minutes per side.

Tender meat does not need to be pounded before cooking. Just press together a little.

Serve with fried onions, sauteed mushrooms and a salad. Instead of sauce, try a seasoned butter.

> HERB BUTTER
> 4 ounces (100 g) butter, softened
> 1 tbsp chopped fresh or 1 tsp dried oregano
> 1/2 tbsp crushed juniper berries
> 1/2 tbsp lingonberries or chopped
>   fresh cranberries
> 1/2 tbsp lemon juice

Mix softened butter with remaining ingredients. Form into a roll, wrap with plastic wrap and refrigerate until needed. This can be made in advance.

Roast Moose

Moose can be roasted just like beef. It should be cooked to "rare" or "medium." The best cut for roasting is the strip loin, but top or bottom round also can be used.

Whichever cut you choose, be sure to use a meat thermometer for best results. A $2\frac{1}{4}$ lb (1 kg) roast, which is enough for 5 people, should have an internal temperature of about 125–135°F (50–55°C) when it is removed from the oven.

Roasting the meat to "medium" retains most of the juices, resulting in a juicy, tasty roast.

Roast moose can be served hot as a main dish or cold as part of a buffet or in sandwiches.

> $2\frac{1}{2}$ lb (1 kg) strip loin, top round or
>   bottom round of moose
> unsalted butter
> salt and pepper
> 2 onions, cubed, or 20 shallots
>
> NATURAL GRAVY:
> 2 cups ($\frac{1}{2}$ liter) stock
> 2 tsp thyme
> salt

Preheat oven to 425°F (225, C). Tie roast at even intervals with cotton string. Brown in butter over relatively high heat and season with salt and pepper. Place onions or shallots in a roasting pan. Insert a meat thermometer and place the roast on a rack over the pan. Roast about 30 minutes, until the internal temperature has reached 125–135°F (50–55°C). Remove from oven and allow to rest 10 minutes before carving.

Deglaze pan with moose stock, then strain. Save the onions to serve alongside the meat. Season natural juices with thyme and salt. If desired, the juices can be thickened with corn starch or arrowroot.

Serve with sauteed mushrooms, a salad, o. fresh vegetables and baked potatoes. Serves 4.

Rustic Moose Ragout

I have never hunted moose, but I know many who have. Therefore, I now and then get a nice piece of meat. To make it easy, and that is always appreciated after a long day outdoors, use tender meat, such as strip loin or top round.

1¾ lbs (¾ kg) strip loin or top round of moose
    butter
1½ tsp salt
1 large onion, coarsely chopped
2 cups (½ liter) mushrooms, preferably wild
1 cup (250 ml) sour cream, heavy cream
    or evaporated milk
young shoots of spruce or barkless juniper

Cut meat into chunks and brown well in butter.

Season with salt.

    Add onion and mushrooms and brown lightly.

    Add sour cream and young shoots of spruce or juniper, which add a taste of the forest. Simmer 10–15 minutes, depending upon the tenderness of the meat. Don't overcook, as the meat should still be pink inside. Salt to taste.

    Serve with potatoes, rice or bread. Serves 4.

Deer

Deer used to be found chiefly in western Norway and along the coast, but now they are inland as well. Although deer are comparatively new to my district, they are abundant. The deer season is at the same time as the moose season, and around here it is usual for the different moose districts also to get a deer quota. But there are some areas that are exclusively for deer.

Deer, also called hart, are probably the most difficult animals to hunt, as they are more aware of the hunter than other game.

It is always a challenge to work with deer meat. The taste is a little bit more pronounced than that of moose, but care has to be taken to preserve its special character.

American elk meat, as well as venison, can be used in these recipes.

Roast Deer

The legs of large animals can be divided along the muscles. It is important to know which ones are well suited to roasting. In order of tenderness, there is top round, the larger section of bottom round, sirloin, the smaller section of bottom round and eye of round.

Many cookbooks recommend marinating game before roasting, but I am a bit skeptical about that, as it is easy for the flavors of the marinade to overwhelm the delicate taste of the meat.

$3\frac{1}{2}$ lbs ($1\frac{1}{2}$ kg) deer roast
butter
salt and pepper
1 onion, in wedges
1 carrot, sliced
$\frac{1}{2}$ celeriac or 3–4 celery stalks, in chunks
5–6 juniper berries
2 tsp thyme

SAUCE:
natural juices
$1\frac{2}{3}$ cups (4 dl) stock or water
salt and pepper
1 tbsp currant jelly
1 tbsp cornstarch dissolved in 2 tbsp
   cold water

Preheat oven to 400°F (200°C). Tie roast at even intervals with cotton string. Brown in butter over high heat. Season with salt and pepper. Pour some stock or water into a roasting pan and add the vegetables and seasonings. Place the roast on a rack over the pan. Insert a meat thermometer in the thickest part. Roast until internal temperature reaches about 150°F (70°C), about 90 minutes. Remove from oven, cover with aluminum foil and allow to rest while making the sauce.

Strain the natural juices from the roasting pan. Add stock or water and bring to a boil. Stir in the jelly and season with salt and pepper. Thicken with cornstarch.

Carve the roast and serve with lingonberry or cranberry sauce, Brussels sprouts, carrots and potatoes. Serves 6.

Leg of Deer

Many people think it is elegant to serve a whole leg. But there is more to preparing this dish than style. The result has to be good, too.

Most deer weigh between 90 and 110 lbs (40–50 kg), so the leg weighs about 16 lbs (7½ kg). When the shank and hipbone are removed, the weight is reduced to about 13 lbs (6 kg), which is around the maximum size that can be prepared successfully in a home oven. Of course, it is possible to get smaller legs, especially from deer calves, and these are wonderful for roasting whole.

1 leg of deer, about 13 lbs (6 kg)
unsalted butter
salt and pepper
1 carrot, cubed
10 shallots, or 1 onion, sliced
1 small leek, sliced
½ celeriac, diced
7–8 juniper berries
2 cups (½ liter) deer stock

SAUCE:
natural juices
1 quart (liter) stock or water
1¼ cups (300 ml) sour cream
1 tsp grated ginger root
3 tbsp lingonberries or chopped fresh cranberries
2–3 tbsp oregano
salt and pepper
cornstarch or flour

Cut off the leg at the knee. Carve out the hipbone, then remove any membranes. Cut off any hanging shreds of meat. Brown in butter and season with salt and pepper.

Preheat oven to 300°F (150°C). Place vegetables and stock in a roasting pan. Place the leg on a rack over the pan and insert a meat thermometer into the thickest part, but be sure that it does not rest against bone.

Baste meat with stock periodically during roasting.

The leg is juiciest when roasted to "medium", with an internal temperature of 135°F (55°C). If you prefer to roast it longer, just follow the table on the thermometer, but it should not reach a temperature higher than 160°F (70°C). Remove from oven and let rest for 15 minutes before carving.

Strain pan juices and add stock for a total of 1½ quarts (liters). Bring to a boil. Stir in sour cream, ginger, lingonberries and oregano. Season with salt and pepper and thicken with cornstarch or flour, if desired.

Serve with sautéed mushrooms, fresh vegetables, such as broccoli, cauliflower, and carrots, and baked creamed potatoes (Page 82).

You can also serve the meat cold, with Waldorf salad (Page 84), sugar-stirred lingonberries, bread and butter. Serves 12–14.

Saddle of Deer

The lower part of the back, called the saddle, is the tenderest part of all animals. The fillet is especially tender and should be removed and used for another dish. It can be difficult to roast a whole saddle, but it doesn't have to be, so long as you know what you're doing. A whole saddle is elegant and can be served either warm or cold. Allow about ½ lb (250 g) per person.

>   1 saddle of venison, about 6–7 lbs (3 to 3½ kg)
>   unsalted butter
>   salt and freshly ground white pepper
>   stock

Carve out the filet and the kidneys, if present. Remove any fat from the underside. Remove all sinews and gristle. Brush with melted butter and sprinkle with salt and pepper. Place on a rack over a roasting pan in a 425°F (225°C) oven until it has a fine brown crust. Reduce temperature to 325°F (160°C). Baste frequently with stock. Esti-

mate a cooking time of 25–30 minutes. Remove from oven and cover with aluminum foil. Allow to rest for 10 minutes before carving.

Loosen meat from the bones. Slice diagonally and return the meat to the saddle.

>   SAUCE:
>   1 quart (liter) stock or water
>   1¼ cups (300 ml) whipping cream or
>   sour cream
>   ½ cup (100 g) unsalted butter
>   cornstarch
>   salt

Deglaze roasting pan with stock or water. Strain into a saucepan. Bring to a boil, add cream or sour cream. Beat in butter and thicken with cornstarch. Salt to taste. Serves 12–14.

Deer Burgers

Ground meat should be made of clean chunks of meat free from membrane and gristle. You can use trimmings and tough pieces from the leg, shoulder and neck. Cuts from these parts are especially good for grinding and they usually need very few additional ingredients to make good burgers. Fry the burgers in very little fat until just cooked through.

Here is a basic recipe for deer burgers.

> 2$\frac{1}{4}$ lbs (1 kg) venison meat
> 5–6 juniper berries
> 2 tsp salt
> $\frac{1}{2}$ tsp pepper
> pinch nutmeg or ground ginger
> 1$\frac{1}{2}$ tbsp potato starch
> 1$\frac{1}{4}$ cups (3 dl) water, milk, or cream
> 1 egg
> oil

Coarsely grind meat with juniper berries. Mix in spices and potato starch alternately with liquid. Add the egg last. Let the ground meat rest for 20–30 minutes for the flavors to blend. Fry a small amount to check the taste, if desired.

Divide the ground meat mixture into portions of about 3 ounces (100 g) each. Flatten and score with a knife. Fry in oil over high heat, but do not burn. Remember that they continue cooking for a while after they have been removed from the heat and therefore don't need to be cooked completely through.

If you plan to freeze the burgers, cool them completely first.

Traditionally, these burgers are served with onions that have been fried until they are golden, soft and shiny.

Serve with a sauce made by deglazing the pan with stock or water and sour cream. Mix in some lingonberries and salt to taste. Serve with a salad.

This recipe can be used for moose and reindeer as well.

Rolled Deer Flank

As with other animals, the flank is good to use for a roll. It can also be ground.

> 1 deer flank, about 2$\frac{1}{4}$ lbs (1 kg)
> $\frac{1}{2}$ leek, finely chopped
> 3–4 shallots, finely chopped
> 1 tbsp salt
> 1 tsp pepper
> 5–6 crushed juniper berries
> 1 tbsp finely chopped spruce shoots
>   (optional)
> 1 tbsp powdered gelatin

Remove all bones, fat and gristle and cut the meat into an even rectangle. Use trimmings in the stuffing. Mix remaining ingredients and spread over meat. Roll up tightly and tie with cotton string at even intervals. Refrigerate overnight.

Roll in cheesecloth and tie both ends. Bring water to a boil and add:

> $\frac{1}{2}$ – 1 tbsp salt
> 5–6 whole peppercorns
> 1 bay leaf
> $\frac{1}{2}$ onion
> 1 carrot

Simmer meat about 75 minutes. Remove from water and place under a weight. Increase the weight after a while, but never use more than 8–10 lbs (4–5 kg). If the weight is too heavy, it will press out all the juice and flavor, and the roll will be dry. Keep the weight on the meat until it is completely cool.

Reindeer

Reindeer is the most important game of our district and the one with the longest traditions. Our cultural landscape shows how important reindeer has been for people, and there are reindeer graves all over the hills. If you look on the map, you will see many names referring to reindeer and reindeer hunting.

Many well-known reindeer hunters come from my district. The best known is Jo Gjende, who has become a legend in these parts.

All this shows just how important reindeer has been as a source of food. Even today, reindeer hunting is a fine way to supplement the larder as well as a sport.

There are both domestic and wild reindeer in the district. For centuries, most of the major wild reindeer herds had their calving grounds in the Smådalen and Veodalen valleys, at the border of Lom and Vågå. This was because of the good grazing fields, as well as the early spring in this region.

Traditions in preparation are much the same as for other meats, salting and drying. If the meat was cooked while fresh, it was usually boiled. Dried meat was also boiled, sometimes along with fresh meat, when available.

Canning was also used to preserve reindeer, and some hunters even brought canning equipment with them, so they could prepare the food before transporting it home, sometimes on horseback, other times on foot.

These traditions regarding hunting and reindeer have given me a special feeling for these animals. Since I know the area where they live, and since I grew up hearing hunting stories and can wander around and see remnants of ancient hunts, it is only natural that I should feel this way. That is why reindeer is one of my favorite foods to prepare. Reindeer meat has qualities and nuances that few other raw materials have. As always, one must vary the method of preparation according to the size and the age of the animal. With careful use of herbs, it is possible to reveal subtle taste nuances.

It is very important to hang reindeer so that it will be tender. Ask your butcher for advice.

In any case, Norway produces large quantities of reindeer meat, so you don't have to be a hunter to get reindeer.

Virtually any big American game can be prepared like reindeer.

Reindeer Tongue Salad

2 reindeer tongues
8–10 juniper berries
2 tsp salt per liter water
water

1 curly endive
orange segments, free from membrane
3 tbsp walnut oil
1 tbsp red or white wine vinegar
1–2 tbsp orange juice

Wash and trim reindeer tongues well and place them with the juniper berries in a pot of boiling, salted water. Simmer, covered, 1 hour. Remove the skin from the tongue and return to water to cool. Carve lengthwise into thin slices.

Arrange endive leaves or other type of lettuce on 4 individual plates. Arrange tongue slices and garnish with orange segments.

Make a dressing of oil, vinegar and orange juice and pour over salad.

Serve with bread. Serves 4.

Another way to serve reindeer tongue is lightly salted with Waldorf salad. The difference is that the tongue is placed in a brine for 2 days before it is cooked.

BRINE
3 quarts (liters) water
scant $\frac{1}{2}$ cup (100 ml) salt

It is also possible to smoke reindeer tongues.

Marinated Cold Reindeer

Use the strip loin from the upper part of the saddle for this dish. You can also use parts of the leg, but then the meat takes longer to marinate.

1 lb (¹⁄₂ kg) reindeer loin
1 tbsp sugar
1 tbsp salt
¹⁄₂ tsp freshly ground white pepper
4 tbsp finely chopped juniper shoots
   (see Page 112)
1 carrot, in matchstick pieces
4 tbsp finely chopped leek
2 tbsp finely chopped mint leaves (optional)

Trim meat of all fat, membrane and gristle.

Combine sugar, salt and pepper and sprinkle half on a dish. Arrange half the vegetables on the seasonings, then place the meat on the vegetables. Sprinkle with remaining seasonings and vegetables. Place a light weight on the meat and refrigerate 2 days.

The peppermint enhances the flavor of the meat.

Serve with a sauce of sour cream and lingonberries, or mix sour cream with berry-flavored yogurt. Serves 6 as a first course.

Roast Reindeer with Raspberry Sauce

The age of the animal is very important in this dish, as is the flavor of the sauce. Moreover, top round has more flavor than loin or filét.

2¼ lbs (1 kg) top round of reindeer,
   preferably from a buck about 1½ to 2½
   years old
unsalted butter
10–12 peeled juniper twigs (see Page 112)

Preheat oven to 475°F (250°C). Brown meat well in butter over high heat. Place meat on a bed of juniper twigs in a small roasting pan. Roast 12–15 minutes. Remove from oven, cover with aluminum foil and let rest 8–10 minutes before carving.

SAUCE:
2 cups (½ liter) reindeer stock (beef can be
   substituted)
⅔ cup (150 ml) crème fraîche (see
   Appendix)
3 tbsp raspberry vinegar
salt
½ tbsp arrowroot or cornstarch dissolved in
   1 tbsp water

Bring stock to a boil and beat in crème fraîche. Reduce slightly. Add vinegar and salt to taste. Thicken with arrowroot.

Serve with fresh vegetables, such as broccoli, carrots, mushrooms and potatoes. Serves 4.

45

Easy Reindeer Stew

There are always bits and pieces of meat which can be used in stews. As far as reindeer is concerned, the simpler the better. Use very little seasoning.

1¾ lbs (800 g) reindeer meat
unsalted butter
salt
1⅓ cups (335 ml) sour cream
8–10 juniper berries
2 onions, in wedges
1 lb (400 g) mushrooms
flour

Use meat from the arm, shoulder or neck. Cut into 1-inch (2 cm) cubes. Brown meat well. Brown only a few pieces at a time, then transfer them to a heavy pot. Season with salt while browning. After all the meat is browned, deglaze pan with water and pour over meat.

Add water to just cover. Add sour cream and juniper berries and let simmer for around 30 minutes, or until almost done. Tougher meat will take longer.

Add onions and mushrooms and cook 10 minutes more. This dish tastes especially good with wild mushrooms. I like cepes the best. If you don't have access to wild mushrooms, cultivated ones will do.

If the gravy is too thin, it can be thickened with flour.

Serve with a salad, lingonberry or cranberry sauce and potatoes. Serves 4.

Rolled Reindeer Eye of Round

This is a slightly different way of preparing rolled meat. I use eye of round from reindeer, moose or deer, however if using deer, be sure to get meat from a large animal. This is a good way to use the toughest part of the leg.

1 eye of round, 1–2 lbs (½–1 kg)
1 onion
¼ lb (100 g) mushrooms
1–2 tbsp parsley
salt and pepper
rosemary
2–3 crushed juniper berries
unsalted butter

Roll out the eye of round by starting with a length-wise cut along one side. Continue cutting and rolling until you have a flat piece of meat about ¼ inch (½ cm) thick.

Finely chop onions, mushrooms and parsley and arrange on the meat. Season with salt, pepper, rosemary and juniper. The amount of filling can vary according to the size of the piece of meat.

Roll up tightly and tie with cotton string at even intervals. Brown in butter, then transfer to a pot of water seasoned with salt, pepper and juniper and simmer until tender. Cool in cooking water.

Slice roll and serve with bread and poached or canned pears stuffed with wild rowan or red currant jelly.

Deer Roll

1 flank of reindeer or other deer
2 tsp mint
10 crushed juniper berries
1 tbsp rosemary
1 tbsp salt
2 tsp pepper
2 tbsp finely chopped onion
4 tsp powdered gelatin

Use the whole side. Remove all bones and membranes. Remove as much fat as possible. Cut into an even rectangular shape. Any trimmings can be used in the stuffing.

Make according to recipe for lamb roll (see Page 123), but use 5 or 6 whole juniper berries in the cooking water, and simmer the roll for about 2 hours.

Warm-Smoked Leg of Reindeer

1 reindeer leg without the joint, around
    9 lbs (4 kg)
  coarse salt

Bone the leg and tie at even intervals with cotton string. Cover with coarse salt and refrigerate 24 hours. Wipe off all salt and ask your butcher to warm-smoke the leg in a 250–300°F (120–150°C) oven until the internal temperature reaches 130°F (55°C) which should take about 1½ hours.

Serve cold, in slices, with mashed potatoes mixed with mashed rutabagas (2 parts potato, 1 part rutabaga), or with sour cream, flatbread and scrambled eggs.

If it is impossible to have the meat warm-smoked, it can be smoked in a regular smoking oven. Preheat oven to 250°F (120°C). Wrap the leg together with some fresh thyme or juniper in aluminum foil. Insert a meat thermometer into the thickest part. Roast until the internal temperature reaches 130°F (55°C).

Dried Reindeer Heart

Butterfly heart and wash well. Cover with coarse salt and refrigerate 2 days.

    Hang the heart in an airy, insect-free place for 10–12 days. Slice thinly and serve with scrambled eggs and flatbread.

Dried reindeer heart can be served just like other air-dried meats. A dried heart weighs 10–18 ounces (300–500 g).

Roe Deer

Roe deer have not been in Norway for very long, thus there aren't so many traditions connected with them as for other types of game. The first recorded observation of roe deer in Norway was in 1864, near the Swedish border.

Even though over 100 years have passed, the roe deer still haven't spread much. It is only in the past 30–40 years that they have increased in significant numbers. It is estimated that there are about 100,000 roe deer in Norway now.

The rapid growth since the last war is probably a result of more modern forestry, with more cultivated fields. There has been an increase in moose for the same reason. This indicates that the roe deer are adaptable, even though they have not spread very far north.

There are no great traditions associated with preparing roe deer, not even in hotel or restaurant kitchens. This is probably because relatively few roe deer are caught, and those that are, are divided among many hunters. It is only in certain parts of Norway that people have experience in preparing roe deer. Few recipes stand out, and even fewer seem to be created especially for roe deer.

Another reason is that roe deer are far down on most hunters' priority list, probably because few are familiar with it, and there is no tradition involved with hunting it, as there is with reindeer and other animals.

In the last few years, some roe deer has been imported from central Europe, which has made it more accessible for restaurants, hotels and home cooks. The price is rather high, so the best way to get it is to know a hunter or to hunt yourself.

Roe Deer Medallions

Use the strip loin from the top part of the saddle. Allow 2 medallions of 3 to 3½ ounce (80–100 g) per person.

1¾ lbs (700–800 g) strip loin of roe deer
clarified butter
salt and pepper

SAUCE:
1¼ cups (300 ml) stock or water
½ cup (100 ml) crèam fraîche (see Appendix)
3 tbsp white wine
2 tbsp black currants
2 tsp mint
3 tbsp butter
salt and pepper

Bone and trim meat. Remove all fat, membrane and gristle. Divide into 8 medallions of equal size.

Brown meat in clarified butter over high heat. Season with salt and pepper. Set aside while making sauce. Preheat oven to 425°F (225°C).

For the sauce, deglaze pan with stock and add crème fraîche and white wine. Transfer to a saucepan and add currants and mint. Stir in 2–3 tbsp butter and season with salt and pepper. When the sauce is ready, reheat the medallions in the preheated oven for 3–4 minutes.

Serve with glazed shallots or pearl onions, sauteed mushrooms and a salad. Baked potatoes taste good with this dish. Serves 4.

Braised Stuffed Leg of Roe Deer

Roe deer has a special taste, which should be enhanced in cooking.

1 leg of roe deer, about 5–6 lbs (2 1/2 to 3 kg)

STUFFING:
1/2 lb (200 g) fresh mushrooms, preferably wild, sliced
unsalted butter
6 shallots, finely chopped
1 tbsp fresh chopped or 2 tsp dried oregano
2 pears, peeled, cored and cubed
1/2 tbsp chopped juniper shoots (see Page 112)

FOR THE POT:
salt and pepper
1 carrot, sliced
1/2 onion, diced
1/2 cup (100 ml) stock or water

SAUCE:
pan juices
1 1/4 cups (300 ml) whipping cream
2 cups (500 ml) stock
1/2 cup (100 ml) white wine
salt
flour, cornstarch or arrowroot

Bone the leg, cutting into the meat as little as possible. With a small, sharp knife and a bit of practice, it is possible to bone the meat without opening the leg.

Sauté mushrooms in butter. Add shallots, oregano, pears and juniper shoots and cook for a few minutes. Fill the leg with this mixture and tie at even intervals with cotton string. Brown the leg quickly in a large pot, and season with salt and pepper. Add carrot, onion and stock and braise over low heat.

Turn and baste leg frequently. After about 90 minutes, it should be done, but it is a good idea to use a meat thermometer and remove the leg when the internal temperature reaches 150°F (65°C). For the sauce, add cream, stock and wine to the cooking liquid and reduce slightly. Strain, and thicken with flour if desired.

Carve meat into thin slices and serve with ginger-poached pears, Brussels sprouts, celeriac sticks and lingonberry or cranberry sauce. Serves 10–12.

GINGER-POACHED PEARS
1 to 1 1/4 cups (250–300 g) sugar
7–8 slices fresh ginger
1 quart (liter) water
10–12 peeled pears (1 pear per person)

Add sugar and ginger to water and bring to a boil in a pot large enough to hold all the pears. Add the pears and place a lid or a dish over them to keep them submerged. Simmer until tender, 5–10 minutes. Cool in cooking liquid.

Deer Chops with Mushroom Sauce

8 chops, cut across the saddle to
    make 4 double chops
unsalted butter
salt

MUSHROOM SAUCE:
1 quart (liter) fresh mushrooms,
    preferably several kinds
butter for frying
1¼ cups (300 ml) whipping cream
3–4 tbsp butter
1 tbsp red currant jelly
salt

Trim chops of fat, membrane and gristle. Sauté lightly in butter until cooked to medium, about 2 minutes per side. Salt to taste.

Slice mushrooms and sauté in butter. Add cream and simmer 4–5 minutes. Stir in butter and jelly and salt to taste.

Serve with fresh vegetables and potatoes. Serves 4.

Pinnekjøt of Roe Deer

Pinnekjøt, dried ribs of mutton, is a specialty of western Norway and appears on many a Christmastable. It is also possible to prepare roe deer in the same manner.

2¾ lbs (1¼ kg) dried ribs of roe deer
barkless birch twigs
water

Since game is generally much leaner than lamb, it only needs 5–6 days to dry. It is therefore unnecessary to soak the meat before steaming.

Cut ribs into chops. Place birch twigs in the bottom of a wide pot, or use a rack. Add water to almost cover the twigs/rack; it must not touch the meat. Place the chops on the twigs and cover. Steam 2 to 2½ hours, making sure that there is always water in the pot.

When the meat separates from the bones, it is ready to serve.

Serve with potatoes, mashed rutabagas, and *lefse* or flatbread. Serves 4.

Bear

Many people wonder how bear tastes. That is probably because of the many stories of bear hunts and the myths surrounding the animal. There aren't many bears in Norway, although the number is supposed to be increasing.

There have been many well-known bear hunters. Among the superstitions associated with bears, one claims that a person is ensured a long and good life by drinking bear blood.

I have been lucky enough to get bear meat a few times. The quality varies greatly, as does the taste, which can range from very pungent to a milder version of the same.

I have made dried ham from the leg, but it was a lot of work to remove as much fat as possible, so that it wouldn't become rancid. Otherwise, I have made dried sausages using an old recipe, and I have made roasts, but they have needed marinating first.

I have received many phone calls from people with a piece of bear meat who need tips on how to prepare it. Here is a recipe to use for bear meat.

Bear Meatballs

14 ounces (400 g) ground bear meat
7 ounces (200 g) ground pork
2 tsp salt
$\frac{1}{2}$ tsp pepper
4 tsp finely chopped fresh or 2 tsp dried thyme
unsalted butter
$\frac{3}{4}$ cup (200 ml) heavy cream
$\frac{3}{4}$ cup (200 ml) stock or water
salt and pepper
thyme
3–4 tbsp port wine

Mix ground meats with seasonings. Form into small balls and brown in butter. Transfer to a pot and deglaze the pan with water. Pour over meatballs and add cream, stock and seasonings. Simmer 15–20 minutes. Just before serving, add wine.

Serve with caramelized pears. Serves 4.

CARAMELIZED PEARS
scant $\frac{1}{2}$ cup (100 ml) sugar
4 tbsp port wine
2 tbsp water
2 pears
sugar

Combine sugar and wine in a saucepan and cook until sugar caramelizes. Thin with water.

Peel and core pears. Halve and thinly slice each half almost completely through, to make a fan shape. Place on a baking sheet, brush with caramel and sprinkle with sugar. Place under the grill 4–5 minutes.

Serve immediately with bear meatballs. Serves 4.

Hare

Years ago, there was always game for sale, and all kinds of birds were popular. Hare, on the other hand, was never considered worth buying, and it usually ended up on the hunter's table.

The hunting methods for hare were the same as for black grouse, and the season usually lasted well into spring. This has varied a bit in our time, and now hare hunting lasts through February. At one time, it ended at Christmas.

In the spring, hare was often hunted when it came into the fields for food. Hunting with dogs was not very popular in the districts. Today most hares are bagged during ptarmigan season.

Just like the ptarmigan, the hare has a natural ability to withstand mold and bacteria, which it gets from the food it eats. For that reason, it can be hung for several days in a cool, airy, insect-free place to tenderize without spoiling. Estimate 5–6 days for a large hare, 3–4 for a small one. Remove the stomach and prop open the cavity with small juniper twigs, to allow the air to circulate. Some do not remove the stomach, though, and I have tried that with good results. Be sure to check if the bladder has been perforated, as sometimes can happen with buckshot. If so, clean immediately, or the meat will be ruined.

Hares can vary from 3 lbs (1½ kg) to more than 9 lbs (4 kg), but average weight is around 5 lbs (2½ kgs). The size varies with when the animal was born, as hares breed several times a year. The first litter can come in February or March, and then others come throughout the spring and summer.

A medium-sized hare serves 6–8 people. To freeze it, skin, divide and wrap as for all other meats.

It is easy to tell the age of a hare by its size. The younger ones are the most tender and mildest in taste.

Roast Hare

1 hare, skinned
unsalted butter
1 cup (250 ml) water
1 cup (250 ml) whipping cream
2 tsp salt
½ tsp pepper
1 tsp thyme
2–3 tbsp lingonberries or chopped cranberries
1 tbsp flour stirred into 3 tbsp cold water

Preheat oven to 400°F (200°C). Remove all membranes from the hare and divide into serving pieces. Brown in butter and transfer to an oven-proof dish. Deglaze pan with water and pour over meat. Add cream, seasonings and berries. Roast in oven until well done, 60–70 minutes. Strain gravy and thicken with flour.

Serve with Brussels sprouts and boiled potatoes. Serves 4.

Braised Saddle of Hare

1 saddle of hare
unsalted butter
1¼ cups (300 ml) mushrooms, preferably wild
about ⅔ cup (1½ dl) whipping cream
3 tbsp lingonberries or chopped cranberries
1 tsp thyme
salt and pepper

The saddle, as illustrated, is the meat between the shoulders and the legs, the section with the chops. Remove all skin and membranes.

Use the remaining parts of the hare for stew or stock.

Brown some butter in a heavy frying pan. Rub salt into the saddle and brown well. Slice mushrooms and brown. Add cream, berries and seasonings. Simmer, covered, about 10 minutes.

Remove meat from bones lengthwise and slice. Serve with potatoes or rice. Serves 2.

Hare Stew

1 hare
flour
unsalted butter
water
salt and pepper
2 tsp cinnamon
2 onions
scant ½ cup (100 ml) sour cream

Divide hare into serving pieces and remove any membranes. Cut out the ribs, as they do not have much meat. Dredge in flour and brown in butter over high heat. Transfer meat to a pot. Deglaze pan with water and pour over meat. Add water to cover. Add seasonings. Simmer 60–90 minutes. Skim. Add onion and sour cream during the last 15 minutes of cooking. Thicken gravy with flour.

Serve with boiled potatoes, vegetables and lingonberry or cranberry sauce. Serves 4 to 6.

Cinnamon is often used in traditional dishes in my home district. I don't know if it was easier to obtain than other spices, but at any rate it has been used in baked goods, porridge, desserts and other dishes. I started using cinnamon with hare in Lom, and I think it is good as well as a bit different.

Game Birds

Nothing tastes more natural and rustic than ptarmigan, black grouse and wood grouse. After a day of hunting, I feel that I owe it to nature to preserve the wonderful flavor and aroma of these birds.

57

Food from the Forest and the Mountain Plateaus

The mountain settlements of Vågå and Lom have rich traditions regarding fish and game. From early times, the mountains provided welcome additions to the larder. Hunting and fishing were ways to supplement the often rather monotonous diet.

Besides reindeer, ptarmigan was most important. Hunting lasted from September until late spring. During the winter, they were caught in traps, while during the fall and spring they were shot with a rifle. There are two kinds of ptarmigan: Mountain ptarmigan is the smaller of the two and lives among the rocks on treeless slopes, while wood ptarmigan lives in the leafy forest. The former is found in my area.

Most of the ptarmigan caught in my district used to be sold to other regions. Most hunters caught more than they needed, and this provided a welcome additional income.

Even though most of the ptarmigan was sold, some still ended up on many a dinner table in the area.

Now, many people regard ptarmigan hunting as a form of relaxation or a hobby. The great quantities of ptarmigan in the old hunting stories are a thing of the past, nothing but a dream for the present-day hunter.

Ptarmigan has a varied diet, according to the seasons, and because of that, the taste varies also. The flavor is best in the fall, when the birds have been able to eat their fill of berries and fresh plants throughout the summer. In the winter, the diet is more monotonous, with birch catkins as the most important food. These give the meat a rather sharp taste.

It is an advantage to know the lifestyle of the animal in preparing game. Every different type gets its characteristic flavor from its diet. My job is to bring out the natural flavor of the game in the best way I can.

When I open the stomach of a ptarmigan, I can see what it has eaten. I think it is important to use some of the same foods that the bird eats in its preparation. That is why I often use berries, such as crowberries and blueberries.

I have used traditional ways to prepare ptarmigan as a departure point for my own development. As additions to these older recipes, I have added new things, which I think go well with ptarmigan, the most important being vegetables, which were rather limited earlier.

Hunting

Anyone with mountain life in his blood can't resist a rainy autumn morning with the fog hanging low over yellow birch trees – or for that matter, sunny days, which make the mountains explode in a feast of color.

Many Norwegians use such days to relax. In wandering around the forests and hills, even the most hard-bitten city person can experience the harmony of nature.

Hunting, no matter what kind of animal, requires careful planning. Dogs have to be trained, tests taken and licences obtained.

TRADITION

Rumors circulate among ptarmigan hunters long before the season begins. Many factors can influence the number of birds from hatching time through the summer. Conflicting reports from the hunting grounds heighten anticipation.

Many people hunt in the same territory year after year. These fall days, with the same hunting party in the same cabin, have become a much-revered tradition for many hunters.

After a few years of hunting, most will realize that it isn't the number of birds in the bag which makes these days special. No, it is the feeling of freedom, the nearness to nature, the evenings by the fire, and everything that goes with it, that makes the experience special.

I associate hunting with my friend Stein, who now lives in the city. For a few weeks with short days and long nights, we rediscover the harmony of our childhood. The walks in wet heather with guns on our shoulders are just as important for a factory worker as they are for a chef.

DIVISION OF LABOR

Food is important to us, and the food we bring with us is chosen carefully. Planning the hunt puts us in the right mood for the big day.

After some years, we have arrived at a good way to divide up the work at the cabin. That is important when both return good and hungry after a long day. I have kitchen duty there, too, for the most part, with Stein not far behind. He prepares the potatoes, sets the table, and brings up cold beer from the cellar.

The exception is when we have bagged hare. Then Stein has the kitchen to himself, while I take care of the day's catch. In the last few years, there has been an increase in the number of hare in the district, so we have gotten some.

IN THE CABIN KITCHEN

We don't always take food preparation very seriously, but some days we return earlier than usual, and then we like to have a good dinner. Other times we have guests, and then I do some cooking.

We like to have game on the menu, and it is extra rewarding to serve game that we caught ourselves. Nature's larders are full in the fall, and there are all kinds of berries and plants which can be picked on the way home. These make the day's dinner varied and interesting.

Duck

One of my favorite foods is duck. I like it roasted until pink, with crispy skin and a thin layer of fat over the breast. I will never forget the duck breast we made at Chez Dominique Toulousy in France, but then we had such big and beautiful ducks there.

Most people feel that there is almost nothing left of a duck after roasting. There are many reasons for this. The ducks in the grocery stores are often small, with little breast meat. Since the best meat sits on the breast, it is very important to buy large ducks. In addition, many overcook duck, which adds to the loss.

Duck is festive food and is often served at holiday time, especially at Christmas. And who hasn't heard of Peking duck, which involves great ceremony to prepare. Real Peking duck requires several days before it is ready to eat. You don't really need to devote that much work and time to get a good result.

Oranges and duck are a classic and tasty combination.

Duck Terrine

1 duck, about 2¼ lbs (1 kg)
1 carrot
½ leek
salt and pepper
2 tbsp chopped tarragon
scant ½ cup (100 ml) white wine

Preheat oven to 425°F (225°C). Remove the skin and cut as much meat from the carcass as possible. Cut into even strips, preferably matchstick pieces. Chop giblets, removing gristle from the gizzard and veins from the heart. Cut carrot and leek into strips. Layer meat, vegetables, giblets and seasonings in a small greased loaf pan. Pour wine over.

Bake about 35 minutes in a pan of hot water. Cool under a weight. Slice. The meat should be pink and juicy.

Serve on a bed of lettuce.

Roast Duck

A duck weighing around 5 lbs (2½ kg) is enough for 3–4 people, but not more.

Wild ducks are usually half that size, so a duck serves 2.

1 duck, about 5 lbs (2½ kg)
salt and pepper
unsalted butter

SAUCE:
carcass, neck, giblets of duck
1 carrot, sliced
1 onion, coarsely chopped
1 leek, sliced
small bunch (100 g) grapes
1 orange, sliced
scant ½ cup red wine
orange juice
grated orange rind
2 tsp arrowroot or cornstarch

Carve out the breast fillets of the duck. Cut off legs/thighs at the backbone. Refrigerate while preparing stock for the sauce.

SAUCE
Preheat oven to 425°F (225°C). Chop the carcass, giblets and neck into small pieces. Place in a roasting pan with the vegetables and brown in the oven. Transfer ingredients to a pot. Add water to the level of the bones. Bring to a boil and skim. Add grapes, orange slices and wine. Simmer 1½ to 2 hours, skimming now and then.

Strain the stock. Add orange juice and rind to taste. Thicken with arrowroot. Add salt if desired.

THE DUCK

Preheat oven to 425°F (225°C). Season thighs and breast fillets with salt and pepper. Brown thighs over high heat and place in the oven for about 10 minutes, while the breasts are being prepared. Brown the breasts as you would a beef fillet, about 3 minutes per side for "medium." Let both thighs and breasts rest 5–6 minutes before carving and serving.

Serve with sauce, fresh vegetables, orange wedges or slices and potatoes. Serves 3.

Small Birds

In speaking of food, we like to compare ourselves with other countries, especially France. In the last few years, we have heard a lot about the "new French kitchen." What this really means to us is hard to say, but it is true that the increased interest shown in food by the mass media has contributed to our awareness and appreciation of good food.

For me, and for other cooks, this increased interest means that we can use our resources better. Unfortunately, we can't always get the same raw materials all year round, but in the fall, most things are plentiful.

Small birds, such as thrush and quail are very little used in Norway, as opposed to the countries of central Europe. In my own district, and probably in others, small birds have been eaten, but there is no real tradition connected with them, probably because of their size. But small as they are, they taste delicious, and in the fall, they are mild, owing to all the berries they have eaten over the summer. Here is a way to prepare small birds, which can be used as a first course.

Sautéed Quail

8 quail
unsalted butter
salt and pepper
$\frac{1}{2}$ cup (100 ml) red wine
$\frac{1}{2}$ cup (100 ml) water
4 tbsp black currants

Wash birds well and dry with paper towels. Tie with cotton string to make them as round and compact as possible. Brown in butter over high heat. Season with salt and pepper. Cover and cook over low heat 5 minutes.

Remove birds from pan, remove string and keep warm until ready to serve.

Deglaze pan with wine, water and berries. Place 2 birds on each plate. Pour wine juices over and serve.

Serve with delicate and pretty vegetables such as cucumber and carrots cut into tournettes, as illustrated, and toast.

Lyons Chicken

In France, this dish is usually made from Bresse chickens, but any chicken will do.

The barley dough in which the chicken is baked gives a subtle natural flavor, which is the idea behind the dish.

2 chickens, about 2 lbs (900 g) each

STOCK:
chicken bones
½ bottle dry white wine
water
7–8 shallots
1 carrot
1 large leek
4 tomatoes
whole white peppercorns
1 small bay leaf
1 tsp thyme
1 tsp rosemary

BARLEY DOUGH:
5 cups (1200 ml) flour
1 ⅔ cups (400 ml) barley flour (found at health food stores)
2 eggs
¾ cup (200 ml) olive oil
½ cup (100 ml) water
salt and pepper

STUFFING:
7–8 shallots, finely chopped
unsalted butter
3 tbsp cognac
4 tbsp chopped thyme
4 tbsp chopped rosemary
4 truffles

SAUCE:
2 cups (500 ml) chicken stock
1 cup (250 ml) crème fraîche (see Appendix)
3–4 tbsp unsalted butter
truffle juice
salt

Bone the chickens, beginning at the back, cutting the breasts off in one piece. Remove the legs/thighs at the backbone and bone them, leaving the thigh and leg meat in one piece. Reserve heart, liver and gizzard for the stuffing.

Preheat oven to 425°F (225°C). Chop chicken bones, place in a roasting pan and brown well in the oven, about 10 minutes. Transfer to a pot, adding wine and water to cover. Bring to a boil and skim well.

Add remaining stock ingredients and simmer 1½ hours. Strain.

Mix ingredients for barley dough. It should be soft and smooth. Roll out to a very thin sheet.

Preheat oven to 425°F (225°C). Place the breasts on the dough. Finely chop chicken livers, hearts and gizzards (remove any veins, gristle, etc.) and brown with shallots in butter. Pour cognac over, light and shake until flames subside. Spread half the mixture on the breasts and sprinkle with half the thyme and rosemary. Thinly slice 2 truffles and arrange slices on the breasts.

Fold the breasts together like a book, and pack the dough tightly around them. Repeat with the thighs. Place on a baking sheet and bake for 35 minutes.

SAUCE
Bring chicken stock to a boil. Beat in crème fraîche and reduce to ⅔ the original amount. Remove from heat, beat in butter, add truffle juice and salt to taste.

Slice chicken and serve with sauce and tournettes of carrots, young turnips, green beans or other fresh vegetables. Serves 4.

Black Grouse

As with wood grouse, the hunting season for black grouse is from September 10 or 15 until Christmas. There aren't so many black grouse in our district as there used to be, but it looks as though the number is increasing. Earlier, they were caught in great quantity, and it was possible to hunt late into spring. Both traps and guns were used. The traps were especially effective in late winter, when the snow melted around the tree trunks and the birds came to eat. It was also common to hunt them at their mating grounds in the spring. Those birds were usually shot.

Black grouse has always been popular in my home area, and it is usually braised or boiled. As with so many other birds, black grouse tastes best in the fall, when food is good and plentiful, and young birds are most tender.

Black grouse is tenderized in much the same way as ptarmigan. Hang the birds by the head in a cool and airy place for about a week. Freeze unplucked.

Braised Stuffed Black Grouse

1 black grouse (pheasant can be substituted)
unsalted butter
water
$\frac{1}{2}$ cup (100 ml) sour cream
salt and pepper
rosemary

STUFFING:
2 apples, peeled and cored
$\frac{1}{2}$ cup (100 g) pitted prunes
$\frac{1}{2}$ cup (100 g) blueberries
heart, liver and gizzard of black grouse
2 tsp rosemary
salt and pepper

Prepare bird for cooking as in introduction to ptarmigan.

Cut apples and prunes into chunks and mix with berries. Dice giblets, removing all veins, membranes and gristle and mix with fruit. Season with rosemary, salt and pepper.

Fill the bird and truss with cotton string. Brown in butter in a heavy pot. When it is evenly browned, place, breast up, on a rack in the pot.

Add water and sour cream to just over the rack. Season with salt, pepper and rosemary. Simmer, covered, over low heat until just barely cooked through, about 30 minutes. Remove bird from pot, and, if necessary, thicken gravy with flour. Salt to taste.

Spoon out stuffing and serve with the grouse. All kinds of vegetables can be used, but I prefer broccoli, Brussels sprouts and carrots.

I think boiled potatoes are best with this dish, but if you prefer another kind, just don't let them overpower the taste of the bird. Serves 2–3.

Potatoes and Salads

Potatoes can be prepared in many different ways. Traditionally, we Norwegians serve boiled potato es for dinner, with little variation. Thanks to the popular press, new recipes for potatoes have reached Norway, and little by little we have learned a number of ways to prepare them.

I still think boiled potatoes are best, especially if they are of good quality. I usually boil them in their jackets for everyday meals, so as not to lose any nutrients. A plain boiled potato is filling, but has few calories. For those who have to watch their weight, that's good to know.

81

Duchesse Potatoes

2¼ lbs (1 kg) potatoes
3–4 eggs
salt
thyme
3–4 tbsp whipping cream
1 egg white, lightly beaten for a few seconds
    with a fork

Preheat oven to 445°F (225°C). Peel potatoes, cut into chunks or slices and boil until tender. Mash or whip, beating in remaining ingredients until creamy. Fill in a pastry bag and pipe 8 mounds of equal size onto a baking sheet. Brush with egg white and bake until golden brown, 5–7 minutes. Serves 8.

Potatoes Au Gratin

¼ lbs (1 kg) potatoes, peeled and thinly sliced
½ onion, thinly sliced
1 tsp salt
pepper
1 cup (120 g) grated Jarlsberg or other yellow
    cheese
¾ cup (200 ml) milk
2 tbsp butter

Preheat oven to 425°F (220°C). Place half the potatoes in a greased ovenproof dish. Sprinkle with half the onion, seasonings and cheese. Top with second layer of potatoes, etc.

Bring milk to a boil and pour over potatoes. Dot with butter. Bake 30 minutes, until the potatoes are cooked and the top is golden brown. Serves 6.

Potato Pancakes

8 ounces (225 g) cream cheese
5 tbsp flour
2 eggs
$\frac{1}{2}$ tsp salt
pepper
$1\frac{1}{2}$ cups (180 g) grated Jarlsberg or other yellow
   cheese
$2\frac{1}{4}$ lbs (1 kg) potatoes
2–3 tbsp whipping cream
2–3 tbsp chopped fresh herbs (optional)
oil

Mash cream cheese with flour, eggs, salt and pepper and stir in grated cheese. Peel potatoes, grate, and stir into cheese mixture. Add cream and stir in chopped herbs, if desired. The consistency should be thick, not runny.

Form pancakes 3–4 inches (7–8 cm) in diameter and fry over medium heat. 3 minutes per side is about right. Turn when bubbles form on the top of the cakes. Keep warm after removing from pan.

This batch makes 18 pancakes, or enough for 6–8 people.

Baked Creamed Potatoes

1 tbsp butter, melted
10 potatoes, peeled and thinly sliced
1 small onion, thinly sliced
$1\frac{1}{4}$ cups (300 ml) whipping cream
salt and pepper
pinch nutmeg

Preheat oven to 400°F (200°C). Brush an oven-proof dish with melted butter. Layer potatoes with onions, sprinkling each layer with salt and pepper. Sprinkle top with nutmeg. Pour over cream to the same level as the potatoes. Bake around 30 minutes, until the potatoes are soft and the top is golden brown.

Salads

A good salad is a fine dish on its own, but many also go well with meat, poultry and fish. Even though the names are the same, salad recipes can often vary from one cookbook to the next. Every cook seems to have his own version.

Sometimes salads seem to drown in mayonnaise. This is all wrong. Mayonnaise should be used sparingly, just enough to bind the ingredients together.

Waldorf Salad

There are numerous recipes for this salad. I don't know which one is the original, but this one should come close.

This is a classic salad from the Waldorf Astoria Hotel in New York. At the turn of the century the hotel had a woman chef, probably the first at such a large hotel. It was she who invented this salad. It is interesting for me to know that Mr. Boohmer, who owned the hotel at the time, was married to a woman named Jørgine, who came from Lom.

8 ounces (250 g) celeriac, or same amount
   celery stalks
2 apples

⅔ cup (100 g) walnuts
½ cup (100 g) mayonnaise
2 tbsp lemon juice
4 tbsp whipping cream
salt

Peel celeriac, cut into even strips and blanch in boiling water. Drain. (If using celery stalks, cut into ½-inch (1 cm) pieces. Do not cook.) Core apples and cut into strips or chunks. Chop nuts and mix with celery and apple. Season mayonnaise with remaining ingredients and fold into fruit mixture.

This salad is delicious with reindeer roast, chicken, turkey or all by itself. Serves 4.

Valencia Salad

½ cup diced or chunk pineapple
1 large apple, peeled and diced
1 large pear, peeled and diced
1 large orange, peeled and diced
1 small bunch grapes (about 4 ounces), halved
   and pitted
½ cup (100 g) filberts
½ cup (100 g) mayonnaise
juice of 1 orange

It is possible to use canned fruit in this salad. Mix fruit with mayonnaise and orange juice. If using canned fruit, it is possible to use the juice or syrup instead of orange juice. Sprinkle with nuts.

This salad also tastes good with chicken or turkey. Serves 4. As a variation, add cubes of cheese for a main dish salad.

Trout in the Green

4 small trout, about 8 ounces (200 g) each
unsalted butter
1 bunch parsley, chopped
1 bunch dill, chopped
salt and pepper
juice of 1 lemon
about ½ cup (100 ml) white wine

Preheat oven to 425°F (225°C). Wash fish under running water and dry with paper towels. Grease an ovenproof dish with butter. Sprinkle half the chopped parsley and dill in the bottom. Season with salt and pepper. Place the fish on the herbs and top with remaining herbs. Sprinkle with salt and pepper. Gently pour lemon juice and wine into the dish to cover the fish. Cover and bake 35 minutes.

Serve with boiled potatoes, a salad and Sandefjord butter (Page 14). Serves 4.

Chives or fresh spinach can be substituted for parsley and dill. It is also possible to prepare 1-inch (2½-cm) slices of larger fish in the same way. Count on one slice per person.

Cold Poached Trout Salad

1 lb (500 g) boneless trout fillet
fish bouillon
3/4 cup (200 ml) sour cream
1 tbsp mint leaves, finely chopped
lettuce
dill, radishes
4 lemon slices

Poach fish using directions from section on fish. Place sour cream and mint leaves in a food processor or blender and process until thick. (Some sour cream will not become stiff, but it is worth trying. Do not be disheartened if it becomes very watery.

It always gets thin before it eventually stiffens. Persevere. Use natural sour cream, without added gelatin.) Refrigerate at least 30 minutes for the flavors to mingle.

Remove any skin and bones from the fish. Place lettuce leaves on 4 serving plates. Arrange fish on top. Garnish with dill, radish slices and lemon. Spoon mint-flavored sour cream alongside. (If runny, serve in a sauceboat.)

Make a salad with the taste of the mountains by placing slices of marinated trout (see Page 21) and slices of roast grouse breast (see Page 76) on a bed of lettuce. Make a dressing of chokecherry vinegar (see Page 118), orange juice and walnut oil.

Desserts

In the autumn, bushes are groaning with berries. It is a good idea to pick them when ripe, to ensure many fine desserts over the winter. This is true for all kinds of berries.

Rustic Dessert

If you're near a forest, you don't have to go to town for berries. With a plactic bag in your back-pack, you can pick the day's dessert on the way home, thanks to nature's bounty.

You can use a mixture of berries. I often use lingonberries, blueberries and crowberries. Place in a pan with a few drops of water and sprinkle with sugar to taste. Cook over medium heat until sugar is dissolved. Remove from heat and add a shot of cognac or preferably aquavit. Serve warm with sour cream.

Blueberries

Every year, masses of berries rot in the forest, but there are those who think about the berries when fall comes. Some have their own special secret spots.

Blueberries are the first berries of the forest to mature. It isn't a good idea to wait too long, as blueberries are very sensitive to frost. In our dis-trict, there are great quantities of blueberries, and I use clear fall days to lay in a good supply for the winter. They freeze very well.

In addition to jam, blueberries can be prepared in many ways: Juice, wine, liqueur, compote, or they can be eaten plain with cream and sugar or even custard. There are endless possibilities. I like to use blueberries to season sauces, primarily with game birds.

If you plan to make blueberry jam, try adding a few cloves. It seemed a bit strange to me, when I first tasted it a few years ago, but now I make it with cloves, too.

Wild blueberries are both sweeter and smaller than the cultivated variety. For cultivated berries, increase sugar in the recipes.

Blueberry Oven Pancake

3 eggs	*pinch salt*
3⅓ cups (800 ml) milk	*2 cups (500 ml)*
1⅔ cups (400 ml) flour	*fresh blueberries*
1 tbsp butter	*sugar*

Preheat oven to 425°F (225°C). Beat eggs. Add half the milk, all the flour and salt. Beat to a smooth batter. Stir in remaining milk. Grease an 12x16 inch (30x40 cm) pan with butter. Pour in batter and sprinkle berries evenly on top.

Bake 30 minutes, until pancake is puffed and firm. Sprinkle with sugar and serve with ice cream or cream. Serves 4.

Grandmother Brimi's Blueberry Pie

Dessert can mean so many things. Some people don't eat much dessert, but it often provides a good finale to a fine meal.

Traditionally, berries have been used for simple desserts like compotes. In my district, pie is rather unusual. I inherited this recipe from my grand-mother, thus the name. She was in the United States several times as a girl, and this is one of the culinary customs she brought back to Norway. Pleasant afternoons eating blueberry pie at her house are among my best childhood memories.

CRUST:

2 cups (475 ml) flour	*½ tsp salt*
¾ cup (180 g) shortening or butter	*5–6 tbsp cold water*

FILLING:

	1 tbsp sugar
1 quart (liter) blueberries	*2 tbsp flour*

Preheat oven to 350°F (180°C). Mix flour, shortening and salt with a pastry blender. Add water and mix quickly until the dough forms a ball. Divide in two and roll out half to a thin sheet slightly larger than the pie plate, and place in the bottom.

Sprinkle with sugar.

Mix berries with sugar and flour and pour into the crust. Brush the edges of the dough with water. Roll out remaining dough and lay on top. Pinch top and bottom crust together. Prick top crust with a fork, so steam can escape. Bake 45 minutes. Serve with cream.

Strawberry or Blueberry Tart

There is nothing we associate more with summer than strawberries. Norwegian strawberries have a sweetness that cannot be compared with those from other countries.

Strawberries are enjoyed in most countries, and the most prized are wild strawberries, tiny but with an intense flavor. These are hard to find.

The French are experts at making cakes with fruit and berries, especially strawberries. One example is strawberry tart. You can use this recipe for other kinds of berries, such as blueberries and cloudberries.

SWEET PASTRY:
3¹/₃ cups (375 g) flour
1 cup (250 g) butter
¹/₂ cup (125 g) sugar
1 egg white
¹/₂ tsp vanilla extract

VANILLA CUSTARD:
2 tbsp powdered gelatin
3 tbsp water
4 egg yolks
³/₄ cup (100 g) confectioner's sugar

1 tsp vanilla extract
3 tbsp whipping cream, whipped

FILLING:
¹/₂ cup (100 ml) strawberry jelly
thin slices of sponge cake
2 cups (500 ml) strawberries, cleaned
*   and topped*

Mix ingredients for pastry and chill 1 hour. Preheat oven to 425°F (225°C). Roll out dough to a thin sheet and place in a quiche or tart pan. Press against the sides and trim edges. Bake until golden, about 15 minutes.

For pastry cream, sprinkle gelatin over water to soften. Beat egg yolks, confectioner's sugar and vanilla over boiling water until thick. Melt gelatin and add to egg yolk mixture. Cool partially, then fold in whipped cream.

Brush the bottom and sides of the tart with strawberry jelly. Cover with slices of sponge cake. Spoon over pastry cream and arrange berries on top. Brush berries with strawberry jelly.

Serve with cream or vanilla custard.

Raspberries

In August, the Norwegian flora starts preparing for the fall. Ripe berries fall to the ground, to make new generations. Many like to gather berries at just that time.

Raspberries are probably the most popular berries we have, and they can be used in many ways. If there are any wild raspberries in your area, it is worth the extra trouble to pick them. They have a sweeter and more delicate flavor and aroma than cultivated berries. You can tell that they have grown in the wild.

If you have enough to make jam, don't use more than $\frac{1}{2}$ cup sugar per pound of berries (200 g per kg).

Botanically, raspberries are related to cloudberries and blackberries. The cultivated varieties are hybrids of many different wild berries.

Raspberries deteriorate rapidly, so act quickly when they're ripe. In addition to traditional dishes, I like to use raspberries to make wine and liqueur, in ice cream or pureed as a sauce, in vinegars and in many more ways.

For a taste treat the next time you serve deer, add some raspberries to the stock for a delicious sauce.

Raspberries are popular in more places than Norway. This recipe for raspberry cream is from the restaurant where I worked in France.

Raspberry Cream

3$\frac{3}{4}$ cups (900 ml) raspberries
$\frac{2}{3}$ cup (150 ml) confectioner's sugar
8 egg yolks
2$\frac{1}{2}$ cups (600 ml) whipping cream

Press berries through a sieve. Measure out 1$\frac{1}{4}$ cups (300 ml) and refrigerate. Beat egg yolks and sugar until thick and lemon yellow. Place over a pot of hot water and beat until mixture is very thick and slightly warmer than body heat. Then beat over cold water to cool down the mixture. Beat cream to soft peaks.

Fold the chilled raspberry puree into the egg mixture, then fold in the whipped cream. Pour into a cold loaf pan that has been rinsed with cold water or lined with sponge cake. Refrigerate 5–6 hours.

Invert onto a serving dish and garnish with fresh berries. Serve remaining raspberry purée alongside. Serves 8–10.

Frozen berries work well in this dessert. Drain them well, or the purée will be too watery.

Warm Berry Dessert

In Norway, we use cloudberries, "the gold of the mountains," for this dessert, but other berries, such as raspberries, blackberries, boysenberries or blueberries can be used.

4 eggs
2 tbsp confectioner's sugar
1²⁄₃ cups (400 ml) unsweetened berries
4 tbsp egg liqueur

Preheat grill. Beat eggs and sugar until light and fluffy. Divide berries among 4 plates. Drizzle with liqueur and spoon over egg mixture. Place under the grill until golden brown.

Serve with vanilla parfait (see Page 98) and wafers (see Page 102).

Prune Cake with Strawberry Purée

1 quart (liter) milk
$^1\!/_2$ cup (100 g) unsalted butter
1 cup (200 g) sugar
2 cups (200 g) flour
6 eggs
$^1\!/_2$ cup (100 g) pitted prunes

Preheat oven to 350°F (175°C). Bring milk, butter and sugar to a boil. Mix lightly together with flour and eggs. Pour into a low quiche form and sprinkle the prunes over the batter. Bake 40 minutes, until golden brown and firm.

STRAWBERRY PURÉE:
1 lb (500 g) fresh or frozen strawberries
1 tbsp confectioner's sugar
$^1\!/_2$ lemon, peeled and pitted

Clean and top berries. Purée with confectioner's sugar and lemon in a food processor. Press through a sieve. Chill, covered, until serving time.

Russian Pancakes

$1^1\!/_4$ cups (300 ml) milk
$^1\!/_3$ cup (70 g) butter
$^2\!/_3$ cup (70 g) flour
2 tbsp sugar
$^1\!/_4$ tsp ground cardamom

3 eggs
2 tbsp ground almonds
butter
jam

Bring milk and sugar to a boil. Cool. Mix together flour, sugar and cardamom and add to the milk. Separate eggs, adding yolks and ground almonds to the milk mixture. Stiffly beat egg whites and fold into batter.

Fry 3 large pancakes in a pan. Layer with jam and top with cream, if desired. Serves 4.

Lingonberry-Cooked Pears

1 lb (500 g) lingonberries or cranberries
sugar to taste
3 cups (700 ml) water
8 pears, peeled, but with stem attached

Bring berries, sugar and water to a boil. Add pears and simmer until just tender. Cool in pan.

Remove pears from pan. Strain sauce and serve with the pears. Ice cream or wafers (Page 102) are good with this dessert.

A little homemade wine or liqueur also tastes good with these pears. Add to the pan just after it is taken off the heat. Serves 4.

Norwegian Pear Dessert

1 quart (liter) water
2 cups (500 ml) lingonberries
sugar to taste
4 pears, peeled, but with stems attached

TROLL CREAM:
1 egg white
2 cups (500 ml) lingonberries (do not substitute cranberries)
3 tbsp sugar

4 cookies formed into cups (see Cone Cookies, Page 104)
6 tbsp egg liqueur

Bring water, berries and sugar to a boil. Add pears and simmer until just tender, 5–10 minutes. Cool in cooking liquid. Halve lengthwise.

Mix egg white, berries and sugar and beat with an electric mixer, until the sugar has dissolved and the mixture is light and fluffy. Spoon into cookies.

Spoon 1 1/2 tbsp liqueur onto each plate. Place pears in the liqueur. Serve cookies filled with troll cream alongside. Serves 4.

Autumn symphony is a dessert composed of cloudberry tart (Page 91), lingonberry-cooked pear (Page 96), filbert cake (Page 98), vanilla parfait (Page 98) and raspberry and cloudberry purées (Page 136).

Filbert Cake

6 eggs
1½ cups (300 g) sugar
1 cup (125 g) flour
1 tsp baking powder
scant ½ cup (100 ml) milk
2½ cups (300 g) ground filberts or hazelnuts

Preheat oven to 350°F (175°C). Grease a 9-inch (23 cm) springform pan. Separate eggs. Beat egg yolks and sugar until thick and lemon yellow. Add flour, baking powder, milk and nuts and mix well. Beat egg whites until stiff but not dry and fold into batter. Pour into pan and bake 30 minutes.

Vanilla Parfait

8 egg yolks
¾ cup (150 g) sugar
1 tsp vanilla extract
2 cups (500 ml) whipping cream

Beat egg yolks, sugar and vanilla until thick and lemon yellow. Stiffly beat cream and fold into egg mixture. Pour into a container, cover and freeze. Serves 10 to 12.

Filbert Parfait Cake

8 eggs
2 cups (500 g) sugar
3¼ cups (400 g) ground filberts
1 tsp vanilla extract
2 cups (500 ml) whipping cream

Preheat oven to 425°F (230°C). Grease a 9-inch (23 cm) springform pan. Separate eggs. Stiffly beat egg whites with 1½ cups (400 g) sugar. Fold in ground nuts. Pour half of the nut meringue into the pan and bake about 5 minutes, until light brown, but still soft. Cool.

PARFAIT

Beat egg yolks with remaining sugar over a pot of hot water until light and fluffy. Stir in vanilla. Whip cream and add to egg mixture. Fold in remaining nut meringue and pour over baked meringue base. Freeze.

Ice Cream Surprise

1 small sponge cake
red currant or other fruit wine
¾ cup (200 ml) whipping cream
1 tbsp sugar
5–6 egg whites
5 tbsp sugar or confectioner's sugar
1 pint (½ liter) vanilla ice cream
berries or other fruit

Preheat oven to 475°F (250°C). Cut sponge cake into slices 1½ inches (3–4 cm) thick. Place in the bottom of an ovenproof dish. Sprinkle with wine. Beat cream with sugar until stiff. Beat egg whites with sugar until stiff. Cut ice cream into thick slices and place on sponge cake. Spread with whipped cream and top with berries. Top with more sponge cake sprinkled with wine. Pipe meringue over the entire cake, covering it completely. Place in the oven (or under the broiler) until golden brown, 5–8 minutes.

Serve immediately, with coffee. Serves 4–6.

Baked Goods

Barley is the most cultivated grain in our district. The type of earth, temperature and water are especially suited to it.

Baking Traditions

Each different area has its own specialties, which are served on holidays and other special days. Here are some recipes for cookies, which still are revered in the Otta valley. Food should both look and taste good, and these cookies are delicate and decorative, as well as delicious. There are a number of country traditions surrounding baking, which has been elevated to a craft in many valleys and settlements in rural Norway. Some of these cookies require special irons. Years ago, these irons were made by local smiths and were signed works of art. Some kinds of cookies are still served in special turned wood plates.

That these recipes call for special irons should not hinder anyone from making them. They won't look quite the same, but they will still taste good.

Wafers

Wafers, or avlettes, are the aristocrat among Otta valley cookies, and they occupy a central place at all celebrations.

The recipes can vary somewhat. Not all use sour cream. Moreover, they are used in different ways in different areas. In my home town of Lom, they are served with sour cream porridge, which is a common first course on festive occasions.

Many homes still have old wafer irons with long handles for holding them over the fire. Now it is possible to buy wafer irons to use on the stove. Local craftsmen continue the tradition of these irons, which have a special pattern.

It is also possible to make wafers on a *krumkake* or *pizzelle* iron.

1¼ cups (300 ml) whipping cream
1¼ cups (300 ml) sour cream
½ cup (125 ml) water
salt
barley flour or regular flour

Combine the creams, then add remaining ingredients. The kind of flour used is a matter of personal preference. In the old days, barley flour was the easier to obtain, but now most use regular flour. Make the batter slightly thicker than for waffles. It is very important that the iron is not too hot. It is a slow process to make these wafers, because the cookies must dry out as well as cook.

Cone Cookies (skryllo)

The people around Otta distinguish between *krumkaker* and *skryllo*, even through both are made in the same iron. Traditionally, recipes containing eggs are called *krumkaker*, while recipes containing cream are called *skryllo*.

2 cups (500 ml) whipping cream   4 tbsp sugar
1 2/3 cups (400 ml) flour   1/2 tsp vanilla

Whip cream and stir in remaining ingredients. Bake in a *krumkake* or *pizzelle* iron and form into cones while still warm.

Rosettes

This is an especially decorative cookie for any coffee table. Rosette irons can be bought in specialty shops. In our district there are many old irons with different patterns.

2–3 eggs
¾ cup (200 ml) milk
1½ tbsp sugar
⅔ cup (80 g) flour
¼ tsp vanilla
shortening or oil

Combine all ingredients except shortening. Heat shortening or oil. Dip the iron in the batter and immediately plunge into the hot shortening. The fat is hot enough when the cookie leaves from the iron almost immediately.

Cook until golden. Drain on paper towels.

105

Simple Wafers

Although these wafers are considered Christmas food in many homes, they often appear throughout the year on coffee tables, much like the cone cookies.

These wafers are usually eaten plain with coffee, but they also can be spread with butter and cheese for a more hearty snack. They usually are served on a plate which is just the right size to fit their diameter of 6 inches (15 cm).

1 lb (500 g) shortening
½ lb (250 g) margarine
1 egg
¾ cup (200 ml) milk
1 cup (250g) sugar
1 tsp hornsalt (see Appendix)
1 tsp cardamom
about 11 cups (1250 g) flour

Cream shortening with margarine. Beat egg with milk. Mix remaining ingredients. Add milk and flour mixtures alternately to the fat. You might want to set aside a small amount of flour for rolling out. Roll out with a patterned rolling pin, then cut into 6-inch (15 cm) circles with a pastry or pizza cutter. Bake on a griddle, patterned side first, over medium heat. Each round should cook 6–7 minutes or they will be soft.

106

Yeast Baking

Many people like to bake their own bread. It is cheaper and healthier. There are certain ground rules to follow in baking with yeast for a good result:

The liquid used in the dough should not be too warm. Fresh yeast doesn't like liquid warmer than body heat. The dough also has to rise adequately. The yeast has to have time to work. It is important that the dough be allowed to rise twice. Don't add all the flour until the dough has risen once. A yeast dough should not rise too long, or it will sink together and the bread will be dry and not very good.

It is usual to distinguish between warm- and cold-rising doughs. When warm liquid is used in the dough, the yeast cells multiply rapidly, and the rising process takes an hour or less. Cold-rising doughs take longer. Room-temperature liquid is used with the cold-rise method, and the dough is not put in a warm place to rise. These doughs can often rise overnight. This is a good idea for coarse, heavy doughs.

Less yeast is needed for cold-rising doughs than for warm-rising ones. Warm-rising is usually used for lighter baked goods, such as white bread, sweet rolls and coffee cakes, while cold-rising is often used for whole-grain breads and Danish pastry.

Basic Bread Recipe

¼ cup (50 g) margarine or 3 tbsp oil
2 cups (500 ml) water or milk
2½ cubes (50 g) fresh yeast
about 7 cups (750 g) flour (use some whole-grain flour for a coarser bread)
1 tsp salt

Water makes bread with large pores and a crisp crust, while milk makes soft bread with small pores.

Melt margarine and add liquid. Heat to body temperature and mix with dry ingredients. If you are using dry yeast, just mix it with the flour. Fresh yeast needs to be mixed with liquid. Reserve a little flour for the second rising.

Knead dough well, cover and set in a warm place to rise. When doubled in size, shape the dough into loaves, rolls, etc. Cover and let rise one more time.

Smaller baked goods should bake at 475°F (250°C) in the middle of the oven, while bread should bake at 425°F (225°C) toward the bottom of the oven. Baking time is around 30 minutes.

Coarse Bread

¾ cup (200 ml) boiling water
¾ cup (200 ml) whole wheat kernels
½ cup (100 g) margarine or butter
1¼ cups (300 ml) water
2½ cubes (50 g) fresh yeast
1¼ cups (300 ml) finely ground 100% rye flour
½ cup (100 ml) wheat germ
¾ cup (200 ml) bran
2 tsp salt
about 5 cups (1200 ml) flour

Pour boiling water over wheat kernels and let soak 30 minutes. Otherwise they are too hard. Prepare a yeast dough by the method mentioned earlier. Let dough rise once before adding the entire amount of flour. Shape into 2 loaves and place in 1 quart (liter) bread pans. Let rise a second time. Bake on the lowest rung in a 425°F (220°C) oven for 1 hour.

Barley Rolls

Barley flour kept many a generation of Norwegians alive in the old days. We don't have to go too far back to find it occupying a central place in most daily diets.

White wheat flour was a symbol of prosperity and progress.

Maybe that is one reason why barley flour has fallen into disfavor.

Now we realize that we need a varied diet, and it is important to use coarse, whole-grain flours.

Barley is an excellent flour and can be used for much more than porridge. Otta Valley Mill in Lom makes excellent barley flour, which I use in these rolls.

1 quart (liter) water
½ cup (100 g) butter
5 cubes (100 g) fresh yeast
2 eggs
3 cups (700 ml) barley flour (found in health food stores)
6⅔ cups (1600 ml) flour

Prepare a yeast dough by the method mentioned earlier. Let it rise well before adding all the flour. Form 24–32 rolls. Let rise until double and bake at 425°F (225°C) in the middle of the oven for 15–20 minutes.

Herbs, Vinegars, Oils

There are all kinds of wild plants that we can pick, and herbs that we can grow. Try growing a small selection to see what you like.

I think wild plants are the most interesting, but not all of them are good at imparting flavor. Dried plants lose their taste quickly, so they shouldn't be allowed to hang too long. Pack them in bags or jars with tight lids as soon as they are dry enough.

I can't mention all the plants I pick and use here. That list would be too long, and that is not my intention. I just hope that my example will inspire others to harvest some of the bounty that nature offers us.

Juniper and Juniper Berries

Few plants have been used in so many different ways as juniper, from beer to cleaning agents. Today, it is best known as the main ingredient in gin and Holland gin. It is also used to flavor game and in smoking meat and fish. But some old traditions still survive, and at Gullhaugen in the Fåvang mountain, an old juniper oil distillery has been restored. In the old days, juniper oil was used as a medicine for rheumatism and colds.

Juniper matures the year after it blooms, when it turns blue. The berries are easy to pick. Dry them in the sun on a damp cloth. When the cloth is completely dry, the berries can be stored in tightly closed jars. Then the berries retain their aroma without becoming hard.

Juniper shoots (the tips of the branches) are also a good seasoning for stock and tea, or in marinating meat or fish.

The best juniper grow high in the mountains.

Birch

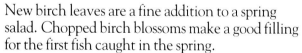

New birch leaves are a fine addition to a spring salad. Chopped birch blossoms make a good filling for the first fish caught in the spring.

Birch leaves can be dried and made into tea, or vinegar can be made with fresh leaves.

I think the best part of the birch is the sap. It can be tapped by cutting a branch on the diagonal and attaching a bottle, or by boring a hole in the trunk and trailing the sap down over a branch to a can. Stop the hole with a cork, when you have collected enough. Then you can return next year.

The best time for collecting sap varies according to the area, but here in Lom the best time is at the end of April, beginning of May.

Aperitif of Birch Sap

Reduce (boil down) sap from $\frac{1}{3}$ to $\frac{1}{5}$ of its original quantity. Flavor with honey.

Cool and serve in a glass or in a carafe with ice.

Another drink is made with 4 parts reduced birch sap and 1 part white wine, or dandelion wine.

It is also possible to make wine and sorbet with birch sap. To store, freeze in milk cartons.

Clover

There are many kinds of clover, but I mean white or red wild clover. Red clover is one of the most important meadow plants, and it originally came to Norway as seeds for pasture. The only difference I see between red pasture clover and red wild clover is that the stalks are slightly different. Clover that grows over a large area often is sweeter than clover grown in a concentrated spot.

It is the honey in the flower, the fine natural sweetener, which makes clover interesting to use. You have to use a lot of blossoms to really taste the sweetness. I make vinegar, I dry clover for tea, and I use it as an herb for marinating meat. Clover gives a lovely taste to birch sap, when cooked together.

Homemade Herb Cheese

It's very easy to make a simple kind of cheese, but few realize that.

This one is rather like cottage cheese, but with a smoother texture. I make it myself, so I can flavor it as I like.

To make this cheese, you need *kefir* (available at some health food stores) or buttermilk and a clean, closely woven cotton handkerchief or piece of cloth. It is also possible to use a coffee filter. Place the cloth in a sieve and hang it over a bowl. Pour *kefir* into the cloth and let it drip overnight. The whey runs off, leaving the curds in the cloth. Use the whey as liquid in bread.

All kinds of herbs can be added to this cheese. I like chives, thyme, mint and dill. You also can add some sour cream or heavy cream to the cheese.

AS DESSERT
Blend homemade cheese with sour cream or heavy cream. Mix with fresh fruit, berries and sugar. For a change, add honey in place of sugar.

AS DRESSING
Thin cheese with some more *kefir* or buttermilk to the consistency of creamy salad dressing. Add chopped herbs to taste.

114

Crowberries

Crowberries are probably the most plentiful berries in Norway. It doesn't have such a strong taste, but it can be used for many things.

I make mostly wine and jelly from crowberries, which I serve with ptarmigan. Crowberries are a regular part of the bird's diet. It is a good idea to add some red currants to the crowberries to encourage fermentation. The wine is best after 2 years in the cellar. Crowberries also make good liqueur.

Crowberry Jelly

3⅓ lbs (1½ kg) crushed crowberries
1 quart (liter) water
1 cup (250 g) sugar
2 tbsp (30 g) pectin

Simmer berries in water 1 hour. Strain first through a sieve, then through a cloth. Cool.

Mix sugar and pectin and stir into the cooled juice.

Heat slowly to the simmering point for 3–4 minutes. Fill in sterilized jars. Makes 6 cups (1½ liters).

Herb Soufflé

Many are a bit nervous about making soufflés, because they deflate so easily. This recipe is easy. If you have never dared, try now.

Most people associate soufflés with cheese. That's true, but it isn't the only way. Many kinds of soufflés are made without cheese. One of my favorites is made with crab and herbs. If you have access to crabs, try a soufflé for a light evening meal.

Remember this rule, which also pertains to other food: The guest should wait for the soufflé, not the reverse.

Melt butter and stir in flour. Cook over low heat 1 minute. Add milk gradually, and continue cooking, stirring constantly, 3–4 minutes. The sauce should be smooth and creamy. Season to taste with salt, pepper and mustard. Add cheese and herbs. Remove pan from heat and beat in egg yolks. Cool 6–7 minutes.

Preheat oven to 400°F (200°C). Beat egg whites until stiff but not dry and fold into sauce mixture. Pour into a greased 1-quart (liter) soufflé dish. Bake around 40 minutes.

Serve immediately with bread.

2 tbsp unsalted butter
2 tbsp flour
¾ cup (200 ml) milk
½ tsp salt
¼ tsp white pepper
½ tsp Dijon-style mustard

½ cup (100 ml) shredded Jarlsberg or Swiss cheese
1 tbsp chopped fresh basil
1 tbsp chopped fresh oregano
3 egg yolks
4 egg whites

Berry and Herb Vinegars

I use a variety of vinegars in my own kitchen, at work and at my cabin. I make these with the different wild plants that grow in my district, along with those plants I grow myself. I use the vinegars for salads, as seasoning for stews and sauces, and in marinades.

I feel it is important to use the natural resources I have all around me, when I serve food from my kitchen. I feel the same way about vinegars.

Nature is full of aromatic herbs and flowers, which make excellent vinegar. Plants that manage to produce fruit in spite of our harsh climate seem to have more taste than similar ones from warmer countries.

Wild Raspberry Vinegar

This vinegar preserves the exquisite taste of wild raspberries.

1 cup (200 g) wild raspberries
3 1/3 cups (800 ml) white wine vinegar (6%)
3/4 cup (200 ml) dry white wine

Clean the berries and place in a jar. Fill to the top with vinegar and wine. The jar must be completely full. Seal tightly and store in a cool, dark place.

After 3–4 weeks, the aroma of the berries will have permeated the vinegar. Strain and discard berries, otherwise the vinegar will taste of pips. Pour into new jars. Vinegar keeps well.

Other Berry Vinegars

Other berries that make good vinegar include black and red currants, wild strawberries and rose hips. Lingonberries are a bit too sour for vinegar. They are much better in liqueur.

Juniper Berry Vinegar

3 1/3 cups (850 ml) white wine vinegar
2/3 cup (200 ml) crushed juniper berries

Bring 3/4 cup (200 ml) vinegar to a boil and pour over berries. Cool without stirring. Add remaining vinegar and pour into bottles or jars. Seal tightly and store 2 weeks before using.

Juniper berry vinegar is good in a mild marinade for hare, for example, because it lessens the sometimes sharp flavor. Otherwise, it is good on autumn salads.

Black Currant Leaf Vinegar

1 1/4 cups (300 ml) shredded black currant leaves
2 3/4 cups white wine vinegar

Bring 3/4 cup (200 ml) vinegar to a boil and pour over leaves. Cool completely. Add remaining vinegar and pour into bottles or jars. Seal tightly and store 3 weeks before using.

Use a small amount of this vinegar when cooking pears with black currants (as with lingonber ry-cooked pears), or use in salad dressing, or deglaze the pan with it after sautéing quail.

Chokecherry Blossom Vinegar

Pick chokecherry blossoms on the day they bloom for the best taste and aroma.

Fill a jar with blossoms. Pour over 4 parts vinegar and 1 part white wine. Seal and store in a cold, dark place 2–3 weeks before using.

You can taste and smell the blossoms in a salad dressing made with this vinegar blended with fresh orange juice and olive oil.

Apple Blossom Vinegar

Many blossoms with intense aroma can be used in vinegar. Apple blossoms are especially good.

Red Clover Vinegar

Another good vinegar is made with red clover flowers. These have a natural sweetness that offsets the vinegar. Late summer blossoms are best.

Herb Vinegars

This is another theme with an endless number of variations. All kinds of herbs can be used.

Birch Leaf Vinegar

New leaves make the best vinegar.

2¾ cups (700 ml) white wine vinegar
1¼ cups (300 ml) chopped birch leaves

Bring ¾ cup (200 ml) vinegar to a boil, and pour over chopped birch leaves. Whisk until cold, using a mixer if desired. Add remaining vinegar, bottle and seal. Store 3 weeks before using. This makes good salad dressing with oil and a little sugar.

Peppermint Vinegar

3 cups (7½ dl) white wine vinegar
1 cup (2½ dl) chopped mint leaves

Bring ¾ cup (200 ml) vinegar to a boil, and pour over chopped mint leaves. Stir until cold. Add remaining vinegar, bottle and seal. Store 2 weeks before using.

This vinegar is good used in dressings for game salads and first courses. It is also good in marinades and with sautéed ptarmigan breast. It accents the natural flavors in a light, icy manner.

Otherwise, you can vary the choice of herbs as much as you like. The basis is the same. Make sure everything is scrupulously clean, or the vinegar will be cloudy.

Aromatic Oils

As with vinegars and liqueurs, it is possible to make flavored oils with all kinds of plants. And the oil preserves whatever is put into it. I usually use olive oil. It is the best, but in the beginning, you can use corn oil, as it is cheaper and easier to get.

Spruce Shoot Oil

Pick the tiny yellow shoots of the spruce tree. Clean well.

1½ cups (400 ml) spruce shoots
2½ cups (600 ml) oil

Fill into a bottle or jar and shake well. Store 2–3 weeks before using. Shake well every other day.

Mix with black currant vinegar for a salad dressing, or saute moose steaks in this oil.

Thyme Oil

1 large bunch thyme
3¾ cups (900 ml) oil

Follow directions for spruce shoot oil.

Use for brushing grilled meat, especially for lamb. This oil is also good in salad dressings.

119

Christmas Food

Christmas has always been a special time. It was not only the people who got something extra. The milkmaid made sure that both large and small animals on the farm got extra food. Even the trolls got a bite to eat. It was for them that the food was left on the table on Christmas Eve.

Butchering time was just before Christmas, and that's when people had best access to fresh food. After the butchering, sausages, rolls and head cheese were made.

It was also a time for baking. In my area, *lefse*, flatbread and other festive breads were always on the table. Baked goods to serve with coffee also have long traditions.

The kind of meat people had could vary, but most had a pig for Christmas, and there was a good supply of game.

It was a matter of honor to have a lot of good food at Christmas, and there were always guests.

Therefore, it is only natural that food was a central part of the Christmas celebration.

The Christmas drink was beer, malt beer in the early days, brewed from old traditional recipes.

Guests came in the evening, and there was usually a table with all kinds of cold cuts and breads. The modern Christmas buffet is a descendant of this table.

At my Christmas table and buffets, I try to combine the old traditional foods with some new things. I have selected some Christmas recipes from those served every year at Fossheim. Most are based on old traditions.

Head Cheese

1 pig's head	15 whole peppercorns
water	15 whole allspice
2 tsp salt per quart	2 bay leaves
(liter) water	5 tsp powdered gelatin
2 onions, in wedges	
8 whole cloves	

Halve head and wash well. Soak in water overnight.

Place both halves in a large pot. Fill with cold water just to cover. Bring to a boil and skim. Add onion and spices and simmer 2½ hours, skimming now and then.

Remove meat from bones. Be sure to discard gristle and glands.

Dip a cotton cloth or a double layer of cheesecloth in cold water and wring. Place in a wide, round bowl. Cover bottom and sides with pork rind. Save some rind for the top. Layer meat and fat. Sprinkle powdered gelatine between each layer. Repeat, ending with a layer of pork rind. Wrap the cloth around the head cheese and tie well with cotton string. Place in boiling water, and let it return to a boil. Simmer a few minutes. Remove from water and cool 15 minutes.

Place under a weight, increasing the pressure gradually, but not exceeding 11–13 lbs (5–6 kg) for 24 hours.

Pickled Pig's Feet

Pickled pig's feet have almost gone out of style. It is an old saying that you drink a shot of aquavit with each bone, and there are 30 bones...

Scald the pig's feet and boil 3–4 hours. Place in a brine of 9 parts water, 1 part salt, a little sugar and vinegar. The feet can be halved.

Serve with *lefse* or flatbread.

Lamb Roll

Use a whole lamb flank for the roll. Remove bones and cut into a rectangular shape.

1 lamb flank, about 2 ½ lbs (1 kg)
2 tsp thyme
½ tsp pepper
2 tsp salt
2 tsp powdered gelatin
2 tbsp finely chopped onion
1 tbsp finely chopped leek

Trim meat to an even shape. Mix remaining ingredients and sprinkle, with trimmings, over the flank. Roll up tightly and tie well with cotton string. The roll should be of even diameter and tied at regular intervals.

Refrigerate overnight for the flavors to mingle.

Wrap roll in a cotton cloth and tie. Place in boiling water that has been seasoned with salt, 6–7 whole peppercorns and 2–3 bay leaves. Simmer 45–60 minutes.

Remove from water and cool 15 minutes before placing under a light weight for 5–6 hours.

Smoked Lamb Roll

Make the roll following the previous recipe. After the roll has been refrigerated for 24 hours, cover it with coarse salt. Refrigerate another 24 hours. Ask a butcher to cold-smoke it for you. Then cook and press as for regular lamb roll.

Lamb Roll with Black Currant Leaves

Use the recipe for lamb roll, but season with the following:

> 2 tsp salt
> 1 tsp sugar
> 1 tsp ground pepper
> 2 tsp powdered gelatine
> 2 tbsp finely chopped leek
> a generous amount of dried black currant leaves

Beef Roll

Ask your butcher for the thin part of the beef flank, or buy a thick flank steak and butterfly it to make a large rectangle.

> 1 beef flank or large flank steak, about 1¾ lbs (800 g)
> 1 lb (500 g) beef, from the flank or arm, cut into strips
> 1 onion, sliced
> 1½ tsp pepper
> 1 tbsp salt
> 1 tbsp powdered gelatin
> 1 tsp rosemary
> 1 tsp thyme

Trim thin flank or butterflied flank steak into an even rectangle. Use the trimmings in the stuffing.

Layer meat and seasonings on the rectangular piece of meat. Roll tightly and tie at even intervals with cotton string.

Prepare as for lamb roll. This beef roll may take longer to cook if it is especially thick.

Lightly Salted Beef Tongue

3 quarts (liters) water
²/₃ cup (150 ml) salt
1 beef tongue,
   about 2¼ lbs (1 kg)

2 quarts (liters) water
⅓ cup (75 ml) salt
4–5 whole peppercorns
2–3 bay leaves

Bring first amounts of water and salt to a boil. Cool. Soak tongue in brine 2 days.

Bring remaining water to a boil, add remaining ingredients plus tongue. Simmer 2 hours. Remove from cooking liquid and peel off skin while still hot.

Brine for Cold Cuts

3 quarts (liters) water
²/₃ cup (150 ml) salt
scant ½ cup (100 ml) vinegar

Combine ingredients, stirring until salt is dissolved. Store head cheese or meat rolls in brine after pressing. They will keep up to 2 weeks. For longer storage, freeze.

Rakefisk (see Page 19)

Coarse Liver Pâté

We eat too little liver, even though it is both inexpensive and nourishing.

The only kind of variety meat people eat is usually liver pâté, and that is almost always bought ready-made. There is nothing wrong with that, for there are many small producers who make good pâté. But why not try making it yourself. Not only is it cheaper, it is at least as good, if not better. And you can season it with your favorite herbs and spices.

There are many recipes for liver pâté, so if you own several cookbooks, you might have a hard time choosing a recipe. Here is a basic one for pâté, which can be varied with different seasonings and different kinds of liver.

1 lb (500 g) liver
½ lb (250 g) fresh belly of pork
1 onion
6 tbsp flour
1½ cups (400 ml) milk or cream (or half and half)
2–3 tsp salt
1 tsp pepper
2 eggs

Preheat oven to 350°F (175°C). Clean liver, removing all membranes and thick veins. Cut liver, pork and onion into cubes. Grind once in a meat grinder. Mix in remaining ingredients.

Many recipes include anchovies, but I use them only rarely. I do like to use thyme to season the pâté, though.

You can make this pâté with a food processor. Then all the ingredients can be combined at once.

Fill into 3 greased 2-cup (500 ml) foil pans or a loaf pan, and bake approximately 1½ hours, depending upon the size of the pans. If you use a meat thermometer, the pâtés are ready when the internal temperature is 155°F (70°C).

This pâté freezes well.

Rolled Eye of Round

1 eye of round, about 4½ lbs (2 kg)
1½ onions, finely chopped
½ leek, finely chopped
2 tbsp chopped parsley
2 tsp rosemary
1 tsp thyme
1 tsp powdered gelatin
unsalted butter

Roll out eye of round with a sharp knife as described in the recipe for game roll on page 46. Try to maintain an even thickness of about ¾ inches (2 cm). Preheat oven to 300°F (150°C). Distribute remaining ingredients over the surface of the meat. Roll tightly and tie at regular intervals with cotton string. Brown well in butter. Wrap in aluminum foil and bake about 3 hours. Cool in foil.

Pork Ribs with Pork Sausages and Meatballs

Pork ribs with sausages and meatballs are the most popular Christmas food in Norway. Norwegian pork ribs consist of the bacon with the rind and ribs still attached, often even with the chops, making for a large piece of meat. There are many recipes for pork ribs, and most include advice on how to get a crispy rind.

My advice is to score the rind 24 hours before roasting, and rub the meat with ½ tsp salt and ¼ tsp pepper per pound (500 g). Refrigerate.

Preheat oven to 350°F (175°C). Place ribs on a rack over a roasting pan and place on the bottom rung of the oven. Roast for 1 to 1½ hours. Increase temperature to 450°F (225°C) and move the roast to the top rung of the oven. Continue roasting for 30 minutes, until the rind is crispy and blistered.

Remove from oven and let rest at least 10 minutes before carving.

Pork Sausages

3¾ lbs (1750 g) boneless lean pork
2½ tbsp (50 g) salt
scant ½ cup (100 ml) potato starch
5 cups (1¼ l) milk
½ tsp pepper
½ tsp ginger
½ tsp cloves
pinch nutmeg
1⅔ lbs (750 g) pork fat

Grind meat with salt and potato starch 3 times in a meat grinder. Mix milk with spices and add gradually, stirring to incorporate. Mix thoroughly.

Grind fat 2 or 3 times in a meat grinder. Carefully stir the ground fat into the sausage mixture. It should be quite smooth.

Fill into sausage casings and tie ends with string. Simmer 15–20 minutes. Season cooking water with the following:

> For every quart (liter) water:
> 1 tbsp salt
> 4–5 whole peppercorns
> 2 bay leaves
> ½ onion

The sausages must not boil, or they will burst. If you like, you can brown them in a frying pan or add them to the roaster with the ribs during the last few minutes of cooking time.

Pork Meatball Mixture

1⅔ lb (750 g) boneless lean pork
1 tbsp salt
3 tbsp potato starch
3 cups (700 ml) milk
1 tsp pepper
ginger, cloves and nutmeg
½ lb (225 g) pork fat

Grind and mix as for pork sausages above. Make meatballs or cakes and fry.

Coarse Christmas Sausage

There are many recipes for sausages such as these. This one contains beef and mutton and is seasoned with ginger.

1½ tbsp salt
1¼ lbs (600 g) boneless mutton or lamb
⅓ lb (150 g) pork rind
1¾ lbs (800 g) beef
¾ lb (350 g) mutton or lamb heart
1 tsp pepper
½ tsp ginger
scant ½ cup (100 ml) potato starch

Sprinkle 1 tbsp of the salt over the mutton and refrigerate 3 days.

Cook rind until tender. It adds flavor and helps to bind the meat together.

Grind meat, rind and heart once in a meat grinder. Mix in spices and potato starch. If the mixture is too stiff, add a little water.

Fill into sausage casings and tie ends with string. Simmer 15–20 minutes. Don't allow the water to boil, or sausages will burst.

Serve with mashed rutabagas and boiled potatoes.

If you leave out the potato starch, you can use this recipe for dried sausages.

Pinnekjøt

Pinnekjøt , dried ribs of mutton, is a popular
Christmas dish in western Norway.

If you plan to prepare the meat yourself, it is
important to chose ribs from a young sheep, or
preferably from a large lamb. If the meat is too
lean, it will be dry.

Sprinkle a layer of coarse salt in the bottom of
a big container. Arrange the mutton ribs on the
salt, then cover with more salt. The meat should
be completely covered with salt. Refrigerate
36–48 hours, depending upon the size.

Wipe off as much salt as possible from the meat.
Hang in an airy place for 6–7 weeks to dry.

Allow 8–10 ounces (250–350 g) mutton ribs
per person. Cut between the ribs into chops and
soak overnight.

Place barkless birch twigs in the bottom of a
large, wide pot, or use a metal rack. Add water
to the top of the rack, but it must not touch the
meat.

Arrange meat on the rack and cover. Cook 2
to $2\frac{1}{2}$ hours. There should always be water in the
pot. The meat is ready when it loosens from the
bones.

Serve with boiled potatoes, mashed rutabagas
and *lefse* , if desired.

Mashed Rutabagas

$2\frac{1}{4}$ lbs (1 kg) rutabaga
3 medium potatoes
milk
meat stock
water
salt

Peel rutabaga and slice. Peel potatoes and cut into
chunks. Cook together until tender. Mash well.
Beat in milk, stock or cooking water from the
rutabagas until creamy. Salt to taste.

132

Sour Cream Porridge

3 quarts (liters) whipping cream
2 cups (500 ml) sour cream (use natural sour
*   cream, without gelatine and stabilizers)*
3 cups (700 ml) flour
¾ cup (200 ml) milk

Bring both creams to a boil and simmer 15 minutes.

Sift in the flour, stirring constantly. It is important that the heat be high enough for the porridge to continue boiling while the flour is being stirred in.

Cook until pools of butter appear. Skim off. Bring milk to a boil and stir into porridge. Serves 10.

Caramel Pudding

½ cup (125 g) sugar
2 cups (500 ml) milk
1 cup (250 ml) whipping cream
4 eggs
3½ tbsp sugar
¼ tsp vanilla

Melt first amount of sugar in a frying pan. Stir until it caramelizes. Pour into a 1-quart (liter) loaf pan, turning it, so that the bottom and sides are covered with caramel.

Preheat oven to 250°F (120°C). Scald milk and cream. Beat eggs lightly with sugar and vanilla. Add to milk mixture.

Place a roasting pan in the middle of the oven and fill ⅓ with water.

Pour pudding mixture into pan and place in water bath in oven. Check to see if pudding is set after 1 hour, but it may take longer.

Cool pudding in the pan, then invert onto a serving dish. Garnish with whipped cream, banana or orange slices, and grated orange peel. Serves 4.

Cloudberry Cream

Cloudberries are hard to get outside of Scandinavia. Other berries can be used in this dessert.

$1\frac{2}{3}$ cups (400 ml) whipping cream
4 tbsp sugar
1 tsp vanilla extract
$1\frac{1}{4}$ cups cloudberries

Whip cream with sugar and vanilla. Pick out a few berries for garnish and fold the rest into the whipped cream. Serve in a bowl garnished with berries. Wafers (Page 102) are good alongside. Serves 4.

Troll Cream

8 egg whites
2 tbsp sugar
1 tsp vanilla extract
2 cups (500 ml) lingonberries

Beat egg whites with sugar and vanilla until stiff. Fold in berries. For a pink dessert, beat everything at once. Serves 8.

Rice Cream with Raspberry Purée

$\frac{3}{4}$ cup (200 ml) whipping cream
2 tbsp sugar
1 tsp vanilla extract
a few drops almond flavoring
2 cups (500 ml) rice porridge

Whip cream with sugar, vanilla and almond flavoring. Mix in the porridge. Serves 4.

RASPBERRY PURÉE
It is easy to make purée of any kind of berries, both fresh and frozen.

1 quart (liter) raspberries
4 tbsp sugar

Purée in a food processor or blender. Sieve to remove pips.

Postscript

What I have tried to express in this book is a summation of the best I have developed in my kitchen over a number of years. You can get many of the ingredients on your own.

In most of the recipes, I have made suggestions for side dishes, but if you don't have the foods in question, use something else. Give the dishes your own personal touch. Maybe they will be even better.

I hope that this book will inspire you to take advantage of the products that nature gives us. Try new foods, study them a bit and plunge in. Maybe this book can be of help.

Appendix

Notes on Ingredients

Certain ingredients in these recipes are difficult to obtain outside Europe. Do not let these strange sounding ingredients intimidate you. Most can be replaced by something easily available in your region.

Cloudberries: These small orange berries, which resemble raspberries, are found primarily in Norway, Sweden and Finland.

They can sometimes be purchased canned or made into jam. Both work well in the recipes in this book, though you will have to decrease the amount of sugar if the berries have been sweetened. You can always use other soft berries in the recipes.

Créme fraîche: Originally from France, this is a slightly soured cream. It lacks the tang of sour cream, so its flavor does not dominate a dish. It does not separate when cooked, so it is excellent for sauces. To make a good substitute for créme fraîche, add 2 tbsp buttermilk to 1 cup whipping cream and allow to stand overnight. Otherwise, you can substitute half cream, half sour cream, or you can use just sour cream. Always buy natural sour cream for cooking. Sour cream with added gelatine and stabilizers is not always reliable in these recipes.

Game animals: Not everyone has access to game. The game recipes included in this book can be prepared with beef, although they will not taste the same. If you are able to get some game, and you are unable to figure out the corresponding type of meat in this cookbook, note the size of the animal or piece of meat and choose the recipe accordingly.

Game birds: The same is true for birds. Pay attention to the size of the bird before choosing the recipe.

Hornsalt: Hornsalt is a leavening agent used in many traditional recipes. Chemically, it is ammonium carbonate, and it was originally made from antlers. It releases an odor of ammonia during baking, but there is no trace of it in the finished product. It makes very crispy cookies. It is a very volatile substance, so shelf life is only about 6 months. Substitute 1 tbsp baking powder for 1 tsp hornsalt.

Leeks: These vegetables look like thick scallions and are wonderful in soup. Substitute onions.

Lingonberries: These berries can be found in jars as compote and jam. They taste a lot like cranberries, but they are much smaller. When substituting cranberries, be sure to chop them first. Cranberries are not suitable in most desserts, where the whole berry is used.

Note: When using the recipes in this book, follow either the cup version or the metric version. Do not mix the two.

Recipe Index